# FESTIVE FEASTS

*Meals and Memories from Halloween to Christmas*

FRONT TABLE BOOKS | AN IMPRINT OF CEDAR FORT, INC. | SPRINGVILLE, UTAH

# FESTIVE · FEASTS

*Meals and Memories from Halloween to Christmas*

## JENI POTTER SCOTT

ISBN 13: 978-1-4621-1725-3

Published by Front Table Books, an imprint of Cedar Fort, Inc.
2373 W. 700 S., Springville, UT 84663
Distributed by Cedar Fort, Inc., www.cedarfort.com

Library of Congress Cataloging-in-Publication Data

Potter-Scott, Jeni, 1965-
Festive Feasts / Jeni Potter-Scott.
     pages cm
Includes bibliographical references and index.
ISBN 978-1-4621-1725-3 (acid-free paper)
1.  Holiday cooking. 2.  Christmas cooking.  I. Title.
TX739.P65 2015
641.5'68--dc23

2015012776

Cover and page design by M. Shaun McMurdie
Cover design © 2015 Lyle Mortimer
Edited by Justin Greer

Printed in China

10  9  8  7  6  5  4  3  2  1

Printed on acid-free paper

# CONTENTS

**THANKSGIVING MENU**

**CHRISTMAS MENU**

# • INTRODUCTION •

*Hi, I'm Jen. I'm a blogger, speaker, author, and lover of all things chocolate and cheese. I have been featured on WowOWow.com, KSL Studio 5, WomansDay.com, RecipeLion.com, ABC4 Good Things Utah, and more. You will find a fantastic collection of my recipes, photos, and humor at Bakerette.com.*

As long as I can remember, my world has revolved around food. I grew up on Mom's heavenly cinnamon rolls and breads, homemade pies, delicious casseroles, and gooey brownies (which I discovered are a health food—if you count mental health, that is).

My introduction to cooking began when I was around 11 years old. Our family hit some hard times and Mom went to work to help support our family. She was home during the day to be with my three-year-old brother and left for work when I got home from school for me to watch him and my eight-year-old sister.

Before Mom left for work, she would set out a dinner recipe and its ingredients on the counter for me to make and have ready for the family when dad came home from work. Mom put a lot of trust in me because there were times when I burned 3,000 calories—that is, I'd forget to take the pizza out of the oven. It was definitely a work in progress and the family was very patient!

Because we hit hard times, Mom began cooking using more of the four basic food groups: canned, boxed, bagged, and frozen. It was cheaper and easier. Her food was incredibly delicious, though. She could turn something boxed into a work of art. However, it wasn't until I lived in Austria in my 20s that I found out there was life beyond casseroles, iceberg lettuce, white bread, American cheese, and processed foods. I discovered spinach, kale, dandelion greens, and spring mix. I gorged on rye bread, semmels, and pumpernickel breads. And, what's more important, I discovered the world of REAL chocolate and cheese—I indulged in more varieties than I had ever imagined! It was almost considered a sin!

My family had lots of food traditions growing up around the holidays, especially around Christmas. Mom would make her traditional Utah Scones for breakfast. The night we decorated our Christmas tree, the family would nosh on toast dripping in butter, which we'd dip in homemade hot chocolate! It was seriously delish! Of course, we also had the traditional turkey or glazed ham for holiday dinners. It wasn't until I married a wonderful cook, whom I call Mr. Chef, that we created many more traditions, many of which I will share with you in this book.

In this recipe book, I will be sharing 80-plus inspired recipes for breakfast, brunch, dinner, and most importantly, DESSERT, accompanied with fun stories to create your own holiday traditions for Halloween, Thanksgiving, and Christmas.

You'll find recipes on how to whip up homemade whipping cream that seriously will stay stabilized for days instead of hours; prime rib so tender it will melt in your mouth; ooey gooey caramel popcorn that will have you licking out of the bowl; and a selection of cookies, cakes, and brownies for Christmas deliveries to your cherished family and friends.

Enjoy the holidays this year . . . Bakerette style!

— Jen

# HALLOWEEN MENU

# Haunting Treats

# Chocolate Pumpkin Spiderweb Tart

Prep time: 30 min
Bake time: 30 min
+ chilling time
Yield: 14 servings

*When I was growing up in Nebraska, we had jumping spiders that scared me half to death: large, hairy wolf spiders up to 2–3 inches across, or so it seemed. I could be exaggerating, but as a young child, any spider looked HUGE. These wolf spiders have keen eyesight, are camouflaged, and spring out of nowhere. I swear they are athletic, breaking all kinds of records in the high jump. Wolf spiders actually don't spin webs, so you're safe to eat this amazing chocolate pumpkin spiderweb tart without something scary jumping out at you.*

## INGREDIENTS

### CHOCOLATE CRUST

1¼ cups granulated sugar

⅔ cup flour

¾ cup unsweetened cocoa powder

Pinch of salt

½ cup butter, melted

### FILLING

1½ cups pure pumpkin purée

¾ cup granulated sugar

4 ounces cream cheese, softened

1¼ cups heavy whipping cream

1 teaspoon grated orange peel

½ teaspoon ground ginger

½ teaspoon ground cinnamon

¼ teaspoon ground nutmeg

¼ teaspoon salt

3 eggs, beaten

4½ teaspoons unsweetened baking cocoa

## INSTRUCTIONS

### CHOCOLATE CRUST

1. Preheat oven to 325 degrees Fahrenheit.

2. In a medium mixing bowl, whisk together all ingredients until well blended. Press dough evenly to the bottom and up the sides of an ungreased 11-inch fluted pan. Place on a baking sheet and bake for 8 minutes or until sides are firm and bottom is slightly bubbly. Cool on a wire rack.

### FILLING

1. Preheat oven to 375 degrees F.

2. Beat together pumpkin, sugar, and cream cheese in a large bowl until well incorporated. Add cream, orange peel, ginger, cinnamon, nutmeg, and salt and continue beating until blended. Add in eggs until combined.

3. Remove ¾ cup of filling to a separate bowl and whisk in cocoa. Transfer to a heavy-duty resealable plastic bag with a small hole cut in the corner; set aside.

4. Pour pumpkin filling into baked crust. Pipe the chocolate mixture in 4 circles about 1-inch apart over the top of the filling. Using a knife, gently drag the knife from the center circle to the outer edge. Wipe clean and repeat around the pie until a spiderweb pattern is formed.

5. Bake for 25–30 minutes or until firm and a toothpick entered in the center of the pie comes out clean. Remove and cool on a wire rack for about 1 hour and refrigerate overnight.

# Chocolate Spider Cake

**Prep time: 40 min**
**Bake time: 20 min + chilling time**
**Yield: 14 servings**

## INGREDIENTS

chocolate cake recipe for two 8-inch round cakes

cream cheese frosting recipe (see below)

20 × 14–inch cardboard or cake board lined with foil

6-inch face mask

one set plastic vampire teeth

8 black or chocolate licorice ropes

2 pastry bags

tip #16 open star

## CREAM CHEESE FROSTING

8 ounces cream cheese, softened

1 cup butter, softened

2 pounds powdered sugar

2 teaspoons pure vanilla extract

purple and orange food coloring

# INSTRUCTIONS

## FROSTING

1. With an electric mixer, beat together cream cheese and butter on medium speed until creamy. Slowly add sugar and beat on low until smooth. Add vanilla and continue beating until well blended.

2. Transfer two-thirds of frosting mixture to a separate bowl and tint with purple food coloring to desired depth of color. Tint remaining frosting with orange food coloring.

## TO ASSEMBLE

1. Prepare a 20 × 14–inch sheet of cardboard by lining with foil.

2. Bake two 8-inch round cakes according to your favorite cake recipe or package instructions. Cool in pans on wire rack for 10 minutes before removing from pan to cool completely.

3. Arrange one cake to the center of the prepared cake board. Thickly frost top of cake with purple frosting and place second cake layer on top.

4. Using tip #16, pull out large orange stars spaced far enough apart around the top and sides of cake. Using tip #16, pull out large purple stars to fill in the rest of the cake.

5. Flatten mask against frosting to one side of the cake. If the vampire teeth are not separated, cut them apart. Insert top and bottom teeth into the cake just below the mask to form the mouth.

6. For legs, insert 4 ends of licorice to the left side of the cake and 4 to the right side of the cake, about one-inch apart. Pipe 8 very large stars to the outside of the cake board to affix the other end of licorice to form the spider's feet.

7. Refrigerate until ready to eat.

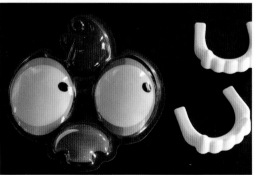

# Witch's Finger Sugar Cookies

Prep time: 20 min
+ chilling time
Bake time: 8 min
Yields: 24 cookies

*The scariest witch ever is the Wicked Witch of the West in the movie* The Wizard of Oz. *This movie was filmed clear back in 1939 and I'm still creeped out by her! Her green skin, pointy black eyebrows, crooked teeth, hunched back, and cackly voice are enough to send me over the edge. I remember cheering when she was mellllllllllting. Witch be gone! These witch's finger sugar cookies are definitely a great depiction of the wicked witch's green fingers!*

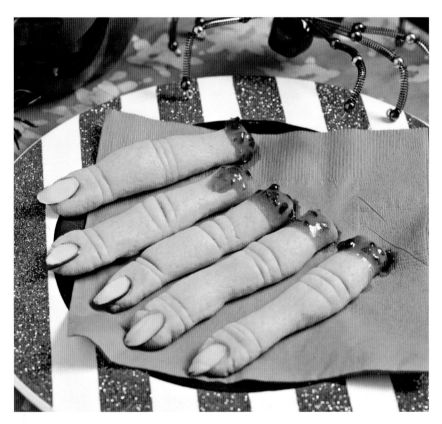

## INGREDIENTS

3 cups flour

¾ teaspoon baking powder

¼ teaspoon salt

1 cup unsalted butter, softened at room temperature

1 cup granulated sugar

1 teaspoon pure vanilla extract

1 egg, at room temperature, beaten

1 tablespoon milk

green food coloring

28 large-sliced almonds

½ cup raspberry jam, warmed (optional)

NOTE: Although this is a basic sugar cookie recipe, do not use store-bought sugar cookie dough. The dough is too greasy to allow this recipe to work its charm.

# INSTRUCTIONS

1. Whisk together flour, baking powder, and salt; set aside.

2. With an electric mixer, cream together butter and sugar until light and fluffy. Mix in vanilla, beaten egg, and milk and continue beating until smooth and well combined.

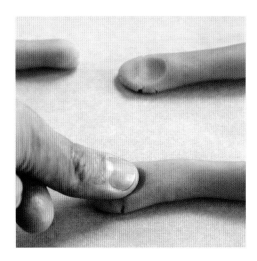

3. Add dry ingredients to wet ingredients in two batches to allow butter to absorb the dry ingredients. After the first batch, add desired amount of food coloring. Start slowly with the electric mixer and gradually increase in speed until thoroughly blended. Add second half of dry ingredients and continue mixing until dough pulls away from the side of the bowl and is well combined. Divide dough in half, wrap in waxed paper, and refrigerate for 2 hours.

4. Preheat oven to 375 degrees F and prepare a baking sheet with either cooking spray, parchment, or a silicone baking mat.

5. Using a tablespoon, scoop up some dough and roll it between a flat surface and the palm of your hand to about 4 or 5 inches long. The circumference should be similar to asparagus (about ½-inch round). Place on prepared baking sheet about 1 inch apart.

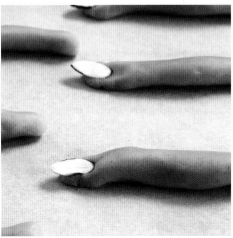

6. Using your thumb, lightly press down on the tip of one end to make an indentation. This is where you will place one sliced almond for the witch's nail. Cut off the other end to make it blunt.

7. Using a paring knife, make several deep horizontal incisions at the center and just below the nail bed—like the marks you have on your own fingers at the knuckles. Make the cuts deep enough so that when they cook and puff, you won't lose the markings, but not so deep that you sever it. Gently press down on the dough on either side of the knuckles to shape the knuckles and make them look large.

8. Bake in a preheated oven for 8–10 minutes or until cookies are slightly golden brown around the edges. Remove from oven and allow to cool a couple of minutes before transferring to a wire rack to completely cool.

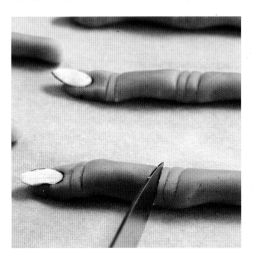

9. Once cooled, dip the blunt end of a finger in warmed-up raspberry jam. Repeat with each finger. Arrange on a platter to eat.

# Caramel Apples

Prep time: 15 min
+ chilling time
Bake time: 5 min
Yields: 6 servings

*Granny Smith apples are the ultimate apple to use for caramel apples. The tart and sour with the sweet and gooey is the perfect combination. Whisk some chocolate on it, too, and you've got yourself a gourmet caramel apple! You know what they say—an apple a day keeps the doctor away. I'm so looking forward to eating one each day.*

## INGREDIENTS

Cooking spray

6 small apples, washed, dried, and stems removed

2 (9.5-ounce) bags soft caramel candies, unwrapped

¼ cup pulp-free orange juice

1 (4-ounce) bar dark chocolate (53% cocoa), chopped into ½-inch pieces (you can also use white chocolate)

assorted small candies, nuts, or sprinkles

6 sturdy craft sticks or popsicle sticks

## INSTRUCTIONS

1. Apples from the store usually have a wax coating on them. Apples should be washed thoroughly to remove the wax before attempting to coat them in caramel. This can be accomplished by dipping the apples in boiling water with a splash of vinegar for a few seconds; remove and thoroughly dry.

2. Prepare a baking sheet with parchment paper and lightly coat with cooking spray; set aside.

3. Insert sticks halfway into the stem-end of apples; set aside.

4. In a medium saucepan, add caramels and orange juice and melt, while stirring occasionally, until mixture is smooth; set aside to cool for a couple of minutes.

5. Grabbing an apple by the stick, dip the apple in the caramel sauce until it completely covers the apple, except for the very top near the stick. Pull up from the sauce and let the excess caramel gently drizzle off into the pan then set apple stick-side up on parchment paper.

6. Place chocolate in a medium bowl and set it over a pan of simmering water to melt; stir until chocolate is smooth and creamy. Quickly drizzle the melted chocolate over the caramel with a fork. If desired, decorate with candies, nuts, or sprinkles.

# Layered Halloween Fudge

Prep time: 15 min
+ chilling time
Bake time: 5 min
Yield: About 2
pounds

*This layered Halloween fudge? Perfection. Anyone who knows me knows I'm a chocoholic. So it should come as no surprise at all that while I was melting the chocolate, I wanted to do a swan dive into the bowl! Chocolate and orange is the perfect combination to get you into the Halloween spirit.*

## INGREDIENTS

1 teaspoon butter

1 cup (6 ounces) semisweet chocolate chips
(I recommend Ghirardelli brand)

1 cup (6 ounces) bittersweet chocolate (about
60% cacao; I recommend Ghirardelli)

1 (14-ounce) can sweetened condensed milk,
divided

8 ounces almond bark

¼ teaspoon orange extract

2–4 drops orange food coloring

## INSTRUCTIONS

1. Line an 8-inch square baking dish with foil, lining the bottom and the sides. Butter down foil and set aside.

2. In a small saucepan over medium-low heat, melt chocolate chips with 1 cup condensed milk, stirring often to make sure it doesn't burn. Pour into prepared baking dish. Place in fridge and chill for 10 minutes.

3. Meanwhile, clean out saucepan and return to stove. Melt almond bark with remaining condensed milk, stirring often to prevent burning. Remove from stove and stir in extract and food coloring. Spread over chocolate layer.

4. Chill in refrigerator for 1 hour or until firm. Grabbing foil by edges, remove fudge from pan. With a sharp knife, cut into 1-inch squares.

# Spiderweb Cookies

**Prep time: 15 min
+ chilling time
Bake time: 4 min
Yield: 24 cookies**

*Coming up the steps from our garden, my daughter and her friend stopped suddenly—there sat a large garden spider motionless on the step, staring them down with its eight eyes. The girls screamed—not just a soft gasp of a scream, but a bloodcurdling scream sharp as needles until I thought my eardrums would burst. I laughed. Why is it that we are so scared of such a small creature? After the girls quieted, the spider remained, daring them to cross her threshold as if they were prey. Being careful not to tear the web design the spider had worked so hard on all morning, I pointed out the beautiful, silky, flat web suspended between the plants the spider had made. These cute cookies are beautifully crafted like the spider's intricate web.*

*You will not find a better sugar cookie recipe anywhere! Not only are these cookies buttery delicious, the dough is an absolute dream to work with. It rolls out easily and is very malleable, and the cookies hold their shape when baked—something many sugar cookies don't do.*

## INGREDIENTS

### COOKIE DOUGH

1 cup butter, softened (use only butter—no substitutes!)

1 cup sugar

2 eggs

½ teaspoon pure vanilla extract

½ teaspoon almond extract

3¼ cups flour

½ teaspoon baking soda

½ teaspoon baking powder

½ teaspoon salt

### ROYAL ICING

1 cup warm water

5 tablespoons meringue powder

1 teaspoon cream of tartar

1 teaspoon clear vanilla extract

2 pounds powdered sugar

black or dark blue food coloring

## INSTRUCTIONS

### COOKIES

1. In a medium bowl, beat together sugar, eggs, and extracts on high speed until light and fluffy.

2. In a large bowl, whisk together flour, baking powder, baking soda, and salt. Slowly stir in wet ingredients with dry ingredients until well combined. Cover with plastic wrap and chill in the refrigerator for two hours.

3. Preheat oven to 400 degrees F. Line a cookie sheet with parchment paper. Roll out the dough to ¼-inch thickness and, using a 4-inch round cookie cutter, cut into circles and place on prepared cookie sheet 2 inches apart. Bake 4 to 6 minutes; transfer to wire racks to cool completely before icing.

### ROYAL ICING

1. In a large mixing bowl, whip together water and meringue powder with an electric mixture until frothy. Add cream of tartar and vanilla extract and mix well.

2. Dump in ALL of the powdered sugar into the meringue mix and beat on low for approximately 10 minutes. (I use my KitchenAid, but a hand mixer will work well too.) The icing will be gooey, like warmed-up honey, and not thick like paste. Use the 10-second rule (see notation below). Check the icing as you go, because you will either need to add additional water or powdered sugar to thicken or thin the icing. Only add additional water 1 teaspoon at a time until you reach desired consistency.

3. Pour two thirds of the icing into a bowl and the remaining amount into a second bowl. Add food coloring to the second bowl and beat well until completely incorporated.

NOTE: Ten-second rule: Lift beaters up from the bowl and drag a knife through the icing and lift up. It should take 10 seconds for the icing to flatten and smooth out. If it smooths out before the 10 seconds is up, it is too thin. If it smooths out after 10 seconds, it is too thick. You be the judge. Once you work with royal icing enough, you'll find your happy medium.

### TO ASSEMBLE

If you've tried cookies like this before, you know just how simple they are to make. And if you haven't, you're about to find out just how easy they are!

1. Using a #6 round tip, pipe an outline on the outer edge of the cookie with white icing. Next, flood the cookie with royal icing right away (flooding means to squeeze icing all over the inside of your outline until it fills in). Once you've filled the whole cookie in, shake it gently left and right to help smooth out the icing. Quickly pipe in a dot to the center of the cookie with black or purple icing, followed by 3 thin graduated outer circles (you can also spiral from center to outside).

2. Using the end of a toothpick, pin, or skewer, quickly drag the tip through the icing, beginning with the inner dot and dragging to the outer side of the cookie. Repeat in round to form a web. Allow to dry completely before stacking or packaging (about 1 hour).

*Have fun experimenting!*

# Super Easy
# Owl Cupcakes

**Prep time: 10 min**
**Bake time: 20 min**
**Yield: 12 cupcakes**

*How many of you remember Halloween as a child? When I was young (waaaay back when), we had these plastic masks with a stretchy string that wrapped around our head to secure the mask. It had slits in the eyes, two small holes for the nose, and a slit for the mouth. Not only was it hard to breathe, but there was no peripheral vision in these masks. As I was running from house to house chasing after my brother (who couldn't care less that I was a football field away), I ran straight into a chain-link fence. \*POW\* and I was down on my back as fast as lightning hits. Instead of seeing birds flying, I swear I saw these owls hovering over my head.*

## INGREDIENTS

1 premade chocolate cake mix or your favorite chocolate cake recipe

12 brown cupcake liners

1 favorite chocolate frosting recipe

24 Oreo cookies, split open with cream filling intact (you should have 12 cream-topped cookies)

24 brown M&Ms and 12 orange M&Ms

## TO ASSEMBLE

1. Make cake according to package instructions. Line cupcake tin with liners and pour batter into individual cups until ⅔ full. Bake according to packaged instructions. Allow to cool completely before generously frosting tops of cupcakes.

2. Split Oreos in half crosswise with a paring knife and retain the cookie with the cream.

3. Using two cream-topped cookies, gently press them (cream-side up) to the frosting, butting them up next to each other.

4. Using some of the leftover frosting, lightly dab a small amount to the backside of a brown M&M and place one to each Oreo half to form eyes.

5. Turning an orange M&M on its side, gently press it down into the frosting in between the cookie eyes to form the beak.

6. Peak the icing a little bit to form a couple of little ears.

7. Repeat for remaining cupcakes.

# Festive Party Starters

# Pumpkin Cheeseball

**Prep time: 10 min
+ 2 hours cooling**

*This is a nice, dense, slightly spicy cheese to serve with hearty crackers or apples. The cheeseball is dense when it's fresh from the fridge, so let it sit at room temperature to soften (about 30 minutes) before serving. You won't be able to dip a cracker or apple slice into the ball for a serving of cheese, so have a spreader handy.*

## INGREDIENTS

2 (8-ounce) packages cream cheese, softened

1 teaspoon onion powder

1 tablespoon dried chives

2 teaspoons paprika

½ teaspoon ground red pepper

8 ounces sharp cheddar cheese, finely shredded

1 broccoli stalk

## INSTRUCTIONS

1. Combine cream cheese, onion powder, chives, paprika, and red pepper until well blended. Stir in shredded cheddar cheese until well combined. Cover and refrigerate up to 2 hours or until mixture is firm enough to shape.

2. Shape mixture into a ball. Smooth the entire surface with a spoon or spatula. Using your fingertip, create vertical grooves in the ball to resemble a pumpkin.

3. Remove florets from broccoli stalk and reserve for another use. Cut stalk to resemble a pumpkin stem and press in the top of the cheeseball. Serve with crackers, apples, or celery.

NOTE: *To make ahead, wrap cheeseball in plastic without stalk and store in the refrigerator up to 2 days. Just before serving, create grooves and attach stalk.*

# Homemade Root Beer

Prep time: 30 min
+ fermentation time

Yield: 40 (1-cup)
servings

*"Double, double, toil, and trouble; fire burn, and cauldron bubble"* (Macbeth, Act IV, scene I). *Halloween just isn't Halloween without homemade root beer bubbling from a cauldron. Make this root beer ahead, place in a plastic cauldron over dry ice and watch the kiddos' eyes grow big as you stir up some spells.*

## INGREDIENTS

1 ounce root beer concentrate

2½ pounds sugar

2½ gallons lukewarm spring water (95 degrees F)

½ (⅛-ounce) package dry active yeast

½ cup pre-boiled water (cooled to 85–95 degrees F)

## INSTRUCTIONS

1. In a large container (not aluminum), add sugar. Shake root beer concentrate really good and mix in with sugar mixture. Stir in water until well combined.

2. In a small bowl, mix together pre-boiled water and yeast and allow the yeast to dissolve for 10 minutes. Add to sugar mixture and mix well.

3. Immediately pour into an airtight plastic bottle (not glass), leaving approximately a 2-inch gap at the top. Cap tightly. To ferment, store in a warm place (70 to 80 degrees F) on its side for 1 to 2 days. Transfer to refrigerator upright for an additional 3 to 4 days. During fermentation, check bottles for pressure. They should be firm when fermentation is complete. Serve cold. Because the bottles have been under pressure, they can overflow when opened.

4. Stores up to one week.

# Magical Disappearing Drink

*This is a fun kids' drink to have at Halloween. You might even want to buy a small "wand" for the kids to stir their drinks as it disappears! There are lots of fun and creative things you can do. The drink turns the color of the cotton candy and has a sweet, bubbly taste!*

## INGREDIENTS

Favorite flavor of cotton candy

11.2 ounces of Perrier or club soda

## INSTRUCTIONS

1. Place cotton candy in a large drinking glass.
2. Pour Perrier or club soda over the cotton candy and watch it disappear!

# Witch's Finger Breadsticks

Prep time: 20 min
+ rising time
Bake time: 10 min
Yield: 4 dozen

*More witch's fingers you say? Yes, you can't have enough witch's fingers or webs during Halloween. These finger breadsticks are fun to dunk in soup and will be a hit with all of your ghouls and ghosts. But you just might traumatize the little witches... just sayin'.*

## INGREDIENTS

1½ cups warm water

1 tablespoon sugar

1 (1/4-ounce) package active dry yeast

4 cups flour, divided

1½ teaspoons salt

48 sliced almonds

1 large egg, beaten with 1 tablespoon water (egg wash)

½ tablespoon sesame seeds

# INSTRUCTIONS

1. In a small bowl, stir together water, sugar, and yeast. Set aside and allow to activate and foam for about 5 minutes.

2. In a large bowl, mix together 1 cup flour and yeast mixture. Beat until well blended. Add 2½ cups flour and salt and beat until dough pulls away from the side of the bowl. If dough is too sticky to work with, add a little flour at a time until it is workable.

3. Oil a large bowl and transfer dough to bowl, turning dough once to coat the top with oil. Cover with a dry towel and let rise in a warm place for an hour or until double in size.

4. Heat oven to 400 degrees F. Line 2 large baking sheets with parchment paper.

5. Cut dough into quarters and roll each into a rope, about 12 inches long. Then cut the rope into 12 one-inch pieces.

6. Roll and stretch each piece of dough until 5 inches long to form a finger. Transfer to prepared baking sheet, lightly cover with a towel, and allow to rise for 15 minutes in a warm place until dough is slightly puffed.

7. To form the finger, pinch each side of the dough to form a knuckle in the center. Using a sharp knife, score lines into the knuckle.

8. Lightly brush each finger with egg wash and press a sliced almond onto one end to form the fingernail. Sprinkle finger with sesame seeds to form "warts."

9. Bake 10–15 minutes or until a deep golden brown. Transfer to a wire rack to cool.

10. Repeat with remaining dough.

11. Serve with your favorite soup or dipping sauce.

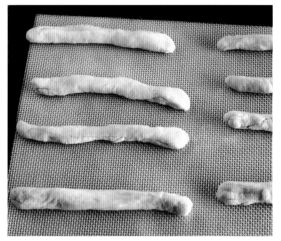

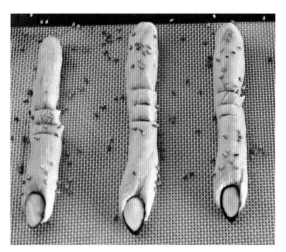

# Salad with Cut-Out Cheese Ghosts and Pumpkins

Prep time: 15 min
Cook time: none
Yield: 4 servings

*I'm a paranormal freak . . . I love watching paranormal shows, but just not any paranormal shows. I like the reality paranormal shows. You know, the kind where they investigate haunted places and try to capture EVP and other phenomena? To freak you out even more, I usually record and watch these shows just before I go to bed. My kids get weirded out when they see me watching these shows in the dark. (But little do they know I hide under my bed covers when I go to bed.)*

*While we're on the topic of ghosts—these ghost and pumpkin cheese toppers are a festive way to dress up your salad. And if for some reason they exhibit any strange phenomena, feel free to call the Ghostbusters.*

## INGREDIENTS

### SALAD

8 cups chopped romaine lettuce

½ cup shredded carrots or matchstick-cut carrots

¼ red onion, thinly sliced

4 grilled skinless and boneless cooked chicken breasts, chopped

4 slices bacon, cooked crisp and crumbled

2–3 Gala apples, cored and thinly sliced (I like to use Gala apples; they don't brown as easily as other apples, which keeps a fresh-looking salad)

¼ cup coarsely chopped pecans or walnuts

4 slices mozzarella cheese, cut with a ghost-shaped cookie cutter

4 slices cheddar cheese, cut with a pumpkin-shaped cookie cutter

### VINAIGRETTE

½ cup extra virgin olive oil

2 tablespoons agave or 3 tablespoons honey

½ cup balsamic vinegar

1 clove garlic, minced or crushed

1 teaspoon dry mustard

salt and pepper to taste

## INSTRUCTIONS

1. Add romaine, carrots, onion, chicken, bacon, and apples in a large bowl; do not mix.

2. Whisk together all ingredients in a small bowl. Drizzle dressing over salad and lightly toss.

3. Divide between 4 plates and garnish with cut-out ghosts and pumpkins.

# Bewitching Main Dishes

# Mummy Dogs

Prep time: 15 min
Cook time: 18 min
Yield: 12 servings

*My older sister and I shared a bedroom and bed when I was little. I was young enough that I was still impressionable and gullible (some would beg to differ that I still am)...I was so gullible when my sister (who's 4 years older than me) informed me there was a "Rock Man" who lived up in the ceiling light cover. Now, let me explain...the Rock Man wasn't some acid rock singer. He was a small man who, when angry, would throw rocks at us. My sister would frighten me and tell me "Look, the Rock Man" and she'd quickly throw the covers over our heads. Pretty soon the Rock Man would pummel us with rocks that would pound my head and body and roll off me. I'd scream out in fear and pain, wishing for it to stop and getting all coiled up in knots. It wasn't until I was older and less gullible that I found out my sister was actually hitting me with her fist and acting like the rocks were rolling off. Yes, I have PTSD and am still getting therapy. Ha-ha. What does this have to do with mummies? Nothing really, other than the fact that it made for a good story and I was tied up in knots like they are.*

## INGREDIENTS

12 hot dogs

1 (11-ounce) can of prepared dough of choice

1 egg + 1 tablespoon water, beaten

mustard and ketchup for serving

## INSTRUCTIONS

1. Preheat oven to 375 degrees F. Preparing baking sheet with a light coating of cooking spray.

2. Unroll dough and use a pizza cutter or sharp knife to cut 12 long, thin strips of dough.

3. Wrap a strip of dough around each hot dog, making sure to leave space at the top to add eyes for the mummy.

4. In a small bowl, whisk together egg and water to form an egg wash. Using a pastry brush, lightly brush the egg over the top of the mummy dog.

5. Bake 18–20 minutes or until golden brown.

6. Before serving, squeeze a little mustard (or ketchup) to make the eyes in the opening you created on the dog.

7. Serve with ketchup and mustard. To make the web, I put ketchup in a small container and made a couple circles of mustard over the top. Using a toothpick, I dragged it from the center to the outside to create a web.

# Award-Winning Slow Cooker Chili

**Prep time: 30 min**
**Cook time: 2–4 hours**
**Yield: 6 servings**

*The fall is full-blown soup weather and I love it. I especially love slow cooker chili. Long-simmering chili, like this slow cooker tailgate chili. Slow cooking is the easiest way to get a full-on flavor and richness that you can't get any other way. This recipe even won a blue ribbon in a chili kickoff!*

## INGREDIENTS

1 pound ground Italian sausage (I like spicy hot Italian sausage)

2 (15-ounce) cans chili beans with juice (chili beans are a mixture of kidney beans, black beans, and pinto beans)

1 (15-ounce) can chili beans in spicy sauce with juice

1 (28-ounce) can diced tomatoes with juice

1 cup beef stock

3 ounces tomato paste

1 small yellow onion, chopped

½ green bell pepper, seeded and chopped

2.8-ounce jar bacon pieces (or bacon bits)

1 teaspoon hot pepper sauce (e.g. Tabasco or Sriracha)

1 tablespoon Worcestershire sauce

### SEASONING

⅛ cup chili powder

2 teaspoons minced garlic

½ tablespoon dried oregano

1 teaspoon ground cumin

½ teaspoon dried basil

½ teaspoon paprika

1 teaspoon white sugar

salt and ground black pepper to taste

### GARNISHMENTS (OPTIONAL)

5-ounce bag corn chips (e.g. Fritos)

4-ounce package shredded cheddar cheese

## INSTRUCTIONS

1. In a medium skillet, crumble ground sausage into pan and cook until evenly browned. Drain grease. Transfer to a 5-quart slow cooker. Add remaining ingredients minus the corn chips and cheese. Stir until well incorporated.

2. Simmer chili on low heat for 4 hours, stirring occasionally. The longer the chili simmers, the better the flavor.

3. Serve warm and top with corn chips and cheese. Or put in refrigerator, warm up, and serve the next day.

# The Great Pumpkin Soup

Prep time: 15 min +
10 min cooling time
Cook time: 1 hour
Yield: 6–8 servings

*Have you ever watched It's the Great Pumpkin, Charlie Brown? Poor Linus; no one believes him that the Great Pumpkin exists and that he will visit the pumpkin patch. Linus is mocked and ridiculed but his belief propels him forward. Unfortunately for Linus, the Great Pumpkin doesn't show—instead, the Great Pumpkin has volunteered to be made into this scrumptious pumpkin soup!*

## INGREDIENTS

6 cups vegetable stock

1½ teaspoons salt

¼ teaspoon each of ground black pepper, cinnamon, and nutmeg

4 cups pumpkin purée

4 shallots, diced

½ teaspoon chopped fresh thyme

1 clove garlic, minced or pressed

5 whole black peppercorns

1 bay leaf

½ cup heavy whipping cream

1 teaspoon chopped fresh parsley (optional)

## INSTRUCTIONS

1. In a large stockpot, mix together stock, salt, pepper, cinnamon, nutmeg, pumpkin, shallot, thyme, garlic, peppercorns, and bay leaf and bring to a boil over medium-high heat. Reduce heat to low and simmer for 30 minutes, uncovered.

2. Remove bay leaf. Let soup mixture sit for 10–15 minutes before transferring small batches at a time (about 4 batches) to a blender to purée until smooth. If you use an emulsion blender to purée the soup, place a towel over the top of the lid before mixing to avoid any accidents.

3. Return soup to pot and bring to a boil. Reduce heat to low and simmer uncovered for 30 additional minutes. Whisk in cream and serve. Garnish with parsley, if desired.

# Ghostly
# Pizza

Prep time: 20 min
Cook time: 5 min
Yield: 6 servings

*During the day I don't believe in ghosts, but at night, I'm a little more open-minded! When I was a child I was afraid of ghosts. In fact, when I was in the dark, I never walked near my bed because my ankles were my most vulnerable part for a ghost lurking under the bed. No, it was always best to run and jump in bed because once there, I was safe. Right? Well, this pizza is like a ghost—watch it quickly disappear.*

## INGREDIENTS

1 pound premade pizza dough of choice

1 tablespoon olive oil

¾ cup spaghetti sauce

pepperoni slices

8 slices mozzarella cheese

1 tablespoon capers

2- or 3-inch ghost cookie cutter

## INSTRUCTIONS

1. Preheat oven to 450 degrees F. Roll dough out into six 7-inch rounds in diameter and about ¼-inch thick, or press and stretch to cover a greased 16 x 11–inch rimmed baking sheet.

2. Lightly brush dough with olive oil and use a fork to prick holes throughout the dough.

3. Evenly divide spaghetti sauce between individual pizzas, leaving a 1-inch border around the edge. Top with pepperoni.

4. Using a 2- or 3-inch ghost-shaped cookie cutter, cut ghosts out of cheese and top over pepperoni.

5. Reduce heat to 425 degrees F and bake pizza for 5–7 minutes. Remove from oven and place capers on each ghost to form eyes. Let stand 5 minutes before serving.

Bountiful Starters

**45**

Entrées Fit
for the Pilgrims

**57**

Rapturous Sides
and Salads

**67**

Sweet Endings

**83**

Thanksgiving
Leftovers

**101**

# THANKSGIVING MENU

# · Bountiful Starters ·

# Roasted Butternut Soup

Prep time: 10 min
Cook time: 50 min
Yield: 6 servings

*Are you going to say a hearty yes to supping on this roasted butternut soup? The answer will definitely be a yes!*

## INGREDIENTS

1 butternut squash (2 to 3 pounds), peeled, seeded, and quartered

2 tablespoons unsalted butter, softened

1 medium onion, finely chopped

3 cloves garlic, minced or pressed

¾ cup shredded carrot

¾ cup peeled, shredded green apple

6 cups chicken stock

nutmeg, cayenne pepper, salt, and pepper to taste

½ cup half-and-half

## INSTRUCTIONS

1.  Preheat oven to 400 degrees F.

2.  Brush squash with olive oil and place face-side up on a foil-lined baking sheet for 45 minutes. Remove and cut into 1-inch chunks.

3.  Melt butter in a large pot over medium heat. Add onion and sauté until soft and translucent; add garlic and cook until fragrant (about 1 minute). Add squash, carrot, green apple, and stock and bring to a boil. Reduce heat to low and simmer, uncovered, for 30 minutes; stirring occasionally.

4.  Remove from heat and let sit for 10–15 minutes before transferring in 4 small batches to a blender to purée until smooth.

5.  Return soup to pot. Whisk in seasonings and cream and warm soup back up before serving. Garnish with parsley, if desired.

# Trish's Hot Spinach–Artichoke Dip

Prep time: 20 min
Cook time: 10 min
Yield: 24 servings

*Have you ever heard the quote "my book club only reads wine labels"? Well, for the book club I belonged to, the quote was "my book club only reads food labels." Book club was all about the food, no doubt. Oh, the books were great, and the company even better, but the food was why we gathered. It was at book club that I fell in love with Trish's hot spinach–artichoke dip served on a platter with delicious crackers and breads. There is nothing else like it! You'll love it too.*

## INGREDIENTS

½ cup butter, cubed

1 medium onion, finely chopped

5 ounces frozen spinach, thawed and drained

14-ounce can artichoke hearts, drained, stems removed and finely chopped

8 ounces cream cheese, softened

8 ounces sour cream

1 cup shredded Monterey Jack cheese, divided

1 cup shredded Parmesan cheese, divided

2 tablespoons green Tabasco sauce

salt to taste

## INSTRUCTIONS

1. Melt butter in pan. Add onion and cook until soft.

2. Stir together spinach, artichokes, cream cheese, sour cream, 3/4 cup Monterey Jack cheese, 3/4 cup Parmesan cheese, Tabasco, salt, and onion mixture until well blended.

3. Spread mixture into an ungreased 9 x 13–inch dish. Sprinkle rest of cheese on top. Bake at 350 degrees F for 10 minutes or until bubbly.

4. Remove and serve warm with crackers.

Prep time: 15 min
Bake time: 2 hours
Yield: 2 dozen

# Bacon-Wrapped Crackers with Parmesan Cheese

*I love this quote by Doug Larson: "Life expectancy would grow by leaps and bounds if green vegetables smelled as good as bacon." In fact, I think someone should come up with bacon-scented candles, deodorizers, and the like. Don't you? These slow-cooked bacon-wrapped crackers make your kitchen smell so good. Bacon always makes it better.*

## INGREDIENTS

1 sleeve club crackers

¾ cup grated Parmigiano-Reggiano cheese

1 pound thinly sliced bacon

brown sugar, to garnish

## INSTRUCTIONS

1. Preheat oven to 250 degrees F.

2. Pour 1 teaspoon of grated cheese onto each cracker.

3. Slice bacon strips in half horizontally and tightly wrap each cheese-covered cracker, being careful not to spill the cheese.

4. Place right side up on a broiling rack to allow drippings from bacon to drain while baking. Bake for 2 hours. The last 30 minutes garnish with brown sugar and continue baking. Serve immediately or at room temperature.

# Lisa's Brie en Croûte

Prep time: 10 min
Cook time: 20 min
Yield: 8 servings

*I went to my niece's bridal shower where her Aunt Lisa served this brie en croûte. Holy COW! The secret ingredient is in the cheese. The brie cheese was warm and gooey and oozed out when cut into. "Sweet dreams are made of cheese. Who am I to dis a brie?"*

## INGREDIENTS

1 (8-ounce) wheel or larger round brie cheese

1 sheet Pepperidge Farms puff pastry, thawed

¼ cup orange marmalade (or marmalade of choice)

1 egg yolk + 1 tablespoon water, beaten

## INSTRUCTIONS

1. Thaw 1 sheet of puff pastry to room temperature (about 15 to 20 minutes).

2. Preheat oven to 350 degrees F. Grease or line a baking sheet with parchment paper; set aside.

3. Unfold thawed pastry. Place marmalade in center of puff pastry. Top with cheese. Wrap pastry over brie and press to seal. Remove any excess pastry. Flip the wrapped cheese over and place on prepared baking sheet. If desired, use excess pastry to decorate the top. Brush entire pastry with egg wash.

4. Bake 20 minutes or until pastry is golden brown. Serve warm with crackers.

NOTE: *Many find the taste and texture of the brie rind unappetizing. To remove the rind, completely wrap the cheese in plastic wrap, freeze for 30-minutes or until stiff to the touch, and then thinly slice off the top, bottom, and sides with a sharp serrated knife. If it is still too difficult to remove, place the cheese back in the freezer for another 30 minutes before trying again.*

# Thanksgiving Sparkling Punch

## INGREDIENTS

½ cup peeled, chopped fresh ginger

½ cup granulated sugar

1½ cups water

4 cups pomegranate juice

4 cups pineapple juice

6 cups ginger ale

## INSTRUCTIONS

1. In a saucepan over medium heat, stir together ginger, sugar, and water until sugar dissolves. Bring to a boil; reduce heat to low and simmer for 20 minutes to form a syrup. Remove from heat to cool. When cool, strain out ginger.

2. Mix together syrup with pomegranate juice, pineapple juice, and ginger ale. Serve over ice.

# Entrées Fit for the Pilgrims

# Cranberry-Glazed Turkey

Prep time: 30 min

Cook time: 2 hours 30 minutes

Yield: 8–10 servings

*I'm not sure where I heard this quote: "In daily life, we must see that it is not happiness that makes us grateful, but gratefulness that makes us happy." When we have Thanksgiving at our home, traditionally we go around the table sharing something for which we are thankful. But not just what we are thankful for, but why! When there is thought behind the statement, it makes it so much more meaningful! One thing I am grateful for is that we always have enough to eat and we've always been able to pay for a bountiful meal at Thanksgiving. This cranberry-glazed turkey is a must-have at our table.*

## INGREDIENTS

### TURKEY

1½ cups butter, softened

32 ounces turkey stock

4 tablespoons butter, softened

14- to 16-pound turkey, thawed

salt and pepper to taste

cheesecloth cut into 17-inch, 4-layer square

4 yellow onions, peeled and quartered

cranberry glaze (recipe to follow)

### CRANBERRY GLAZE

1 tablespoon butter

¼ cup yellow onion

pinch of garlic powder

2 sage leaves

1 cup cranberries

⅔ cup honey

⅔ cup apple cider, plus more if needed

½ cup cranberry jelly

¼ teaspoon salt

a pinch of ground black pepper

# INSTRUCTIONS

## TURKEY

1. Place oven rack to lowest level. Preheat oven to 450 degrees F. In a large saucepan over medium heat, melt butter and add turkey stock. Turn off heat to keep warm. Immerse cheesecloth in butter–turkey stock mixture, cover, and set aside to soak.

2. Place turkey on a work surface and season inside of cavity with salt and pepper. Fold wing tips under. If desired, fill cavity and neck cavity with stuffing. Loosely tie legs together with kitchen twine. Rub turkey with 4 tablespoons of butter and season with salt and pepper to taste.

3. Spread quartered onions in a roasting pan and transfer turkey on top of onions.

4. Remove cheesecloth from liquid and lightly squeeze leaving enough liquid on cheesecloth to keep it very damp. Lay it evenly over breast and leg. Roast for 30 minutes, then reduce heat to 350 degrees F.

5. Pour ¼ of turkey stock over cheesecloth and exposed parts of turkey and continue roasting, basting every 30 minutes for about 2 hours more.

6. When turkey stock is all gone, remove cheesecloth from turkey and discard. Continue cooking until a meat thermometer registers 155 degrees F when inserted into the thickest part of the thigh (avoiding the bone).

7. Brush cranberry glaze all over turkey and roast for 10 to 15 minutes more. Coat turkey with more glaze and cook until a thermometer registers 165 degrees F.

8. Remove from oven, cover with foil, and let rest for about 15 minutes before carving.

## CRANBERRY GLAZE

1. In a medium saucepan over medium heat, melt butter. Add onion and sauté until translucent. Add garlic powder and sage leaves and cook for one minute more before adding cranberries, honey, apple cider, jelly, salt, and pepper. Increase heat to medium-high and simmer until cranberries are ready to burst (about 3 minutes).

2. Transfer to a blender and purée until smooth. Pour back into a small saucepan through a fine sieve and reduce juice over medium heat until thickened (about 10 to 15 minutes), stirring occasionally. Juice should be reduced to about 1¼ cups. If it seems too thick, you can thin it with more apple cider.

# Herb-Roasted Chicken with Vegetables

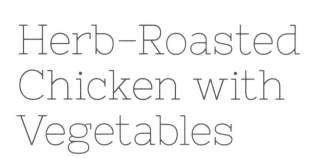

*If you aren't a turkey eater, try this herb-roasted chicken with vegetables. It's a simple dish made out of an herbed butter rub that really tenderizes the chicken.*

## INGREDIENTS

### HERBED BUTTER RUB

9 tablespoons unsalted butter at room temperature

3 teaspoons chopped fresh rosemary

3 teaspoons chopped fresh thyme

½ teaspoon fresh lemon juice

½ teaspoon salt

½ teaspoon ground black pepper

3 garlic cloves, minced or pressed

### CHICKEN

One 3- or 4-pound chicken, thawed

salt and ground black pepper to taste

5 sprigs fresh rosemary

5 sprigs fresh thyme

½ lemon, halved

### VEGETABLES

6 baby red potatoes, halved

4 medium carrots, peeled and halved lengthwise

1 small onion, peeled, halved, and quartered

1 cup chicken broth

3 tablespoons herbed butter rub, melted

## INSTRUCTIONS

1. Preheat oven to 400 degrees F. Line a roasting pan with foil; set aside.

2. For herbed butter: In a small bowl, mix together all ingredients until smooth and creamy.

3. For chicken: Tuck wings under chicken and sprinkle the cavity with salt and pepper. Add 2 tablespoons of herbed butter and rub into the cavity. Insert rosemary, thyme, and lemon in the cavity. Tie legs loosely

together with kitchen twine. Rub 4 tablespoons of herbed butter all over the outside and under the skin of the chicken without tearing the skin. Place chicken in prepared roasting pan.

4. For vegetables: Toss together potatoes, carrots, onion, and herbed butter until well coated. Arrange vegetables around chicken in a single layer. Add broth to the bottom of the pan. Roast chicken uncovered until a meat thermometer inserted into the thickest part of the chicken thigh (not touching bone) registers between 160–165 degrees F (about 1½ hours). Remove chicken, cover, and let rest for 20 minutes before carving.

5. Transfer vegetables to a dish and serve with the chicken.

# Tangy Orange Cornish Game Hens

Prep time: 30 min

Cook time: 1 hour

Yield: 6 hens

*My husband introduced me to Cornish game hens. I had never eaten one before, and when I saw them, I thought they were the cutest things ever! Little versions are always so adorable, don't you think? Although we traditionally have turkey each Thanksgiving, one year when the kids were young we each had our own little "turkey"... we made individualized Cornish game hens. We stuffed them and cooked them just as we would a turkey. The tangy orange recipe is one we love. It has a little zing to it.*

## INGREDIENTS

6 frozen Cornish game hens, thawed

2 tablespoons olive oil

1 tablespoon salt

1 teaspoon ground black pepper

1 tablespoon poultry seasoning

1 bell pepper, chopped

½ onion, chopped

2 celery stalks, chopped

### SAUCE

2 medium-sized navel oranges, juiced (about 4 ounces juice)

1 orange, zested

6 tablespoons brown sugar

1 tablespoon molasses

1 clove garlic, minced or pressed

½ tablespoon hot sauce

¼ to ½ teaspoon crushed red pepper

2 teaspoons cornstarch

4 teaspoons water

## INSTRUCTIONS

1. Preheat oven to 350 degrees F. Line a baking sheet with foil; set aside.

2. Brush olive oil all over the outsides of the hens.

3. Mix together salt, pepper, and poultry season. Generously season the insides and outsides of hens.

4. Loosely stuff the insides of hens with bell pepper, onion, and celery. Place on the prepared baking sheet with plenty of space between them (you may need to use two pans).

5. Bake for one hour or until an instant-read thermometer inserted into the thickest part of the thigh registers 165 degrees F and the juices run clear. The last 15 minutes of baking, brush hens with the orange sauce every five minutes until hens are done. Remove from oven, loosely tent with foil, and let rest 10 minutes before carving or serving.

## SAUCE

1. In a small saucepan, whisk together orange juice, brown sugar, molasses, garlic, hot sauce, and red pepper. Bring to boil over medium-high heat for 2 minutes, stirring in between. Dissolve cornstarch in water and add to sauce. Continue to boil on medium-high heat for 30–45 seconds or until the sauce thickens to coat the spoon. Remove from heat and stir in orange zest.

# Rapturous Sides and Salads

# Aunt Lani's Yeast Rolls

**Prep time: 5 min + 2 hours 15 min rising time**

**Bake time: 15 min**

**Yield: 25 rolls**

*It seems many a meal is judged by the bread! If you serve my aunt's yeast rolls at Thanksgiving, your meal will be judged superbly!*

## INGREDIENTS

1½ cups milk, scalded

½ cup sugar

2 teaspoons salt

¼ cup shortening

2 (¾-ounce) packages yeast

½ cup lukewarm water

2 eggs, beaten

5½ cups flour, divided

## INSTRUCTIONS

1. In a small saucepan, scald milk over medium high heat (about 180 degrees F), stirring occasionally. Remove from burner and add sugar, salt, and shortening. Set aside and cool until mixture is lukewarm.

2. Meanwhile, in a small bowl, mix together yeast in water; set aside to activate (about 5 minutes).

3. In a large mixing bowl, stir together milk mixture and 2 cups flour until well combined.

4. Add eggs to yeast mixture, fold into flour mixture, and beat well. Add 3 cups flour and continue mixing.

5. Turn out onto a floured surface and knead for approximately 5 minutes, adding remaining flour as needed until dough is smooth and elastic. Place in a well-greased bowl, turning once in the bowl to grease the top. Cover with a damp cloth and set in a warm place to rise for about 1½ hours or until double in size.

6. Punch down dough, shape into rolls as desired, and place on a greased baking sheet. Set in a warm place to rise for about 45 minutes or until double in size.

7. Preheat oven to 350 degrees F. Bake for 15–20 minutes.

NOTE: *When adding flour, it is best to spoon flour into the measuring cup and then level it off so it isn't compact. This makes for a better roll.*

# Butternut-Potato Gratin

**Prep time:** 25 min
**Bake time:** 1½ hours

*It's the surprising and unexpected combinations of ingredients that make cooking so satisfying. Who knew that butternut squash, ground nutmeg, and Fontina cheese could turn regular au gratin potatoes into something spectacular and oh-so-flavorful?*

## INGREDIENTS

2 large or 3 medium Yukon Gold potatoes, washed, blemishes removed, and thinly sliced (skin attached)

½ pound butternut squash, peeled, halved, seeded, and thinly sliced crosswise

4 green onions, sliced

1 tablespoon snipped fresh sage

4 cloves garlic, minced or pressed

1 teaspoon salt

2 teaspoons ground nutmeg

2 teaspoons ground black pepper

5 ounces Fontina cheese, shredded (about 1½ cups; if you can't find Fontina cheese, substitute with provolone, Gruyère, or Gouda cheese)

1½ cups whipping cream

## INSTRUCTIONS

1. Preheat oven to 350 degrees F. Grease the inside of a 2-quart casserole dish.

2. Line the dish with half of the potato slices, butternut squash, and leeks (in that order). Top with half of the sage, half of the garlic, half of the salt, half of the ground pepper, and half of the cheese. Repeat layers. Pour cream over the top.

3. Cover with foil. Bake for 1 hour 20 minutes, uncover, and bake an additional 10 minutes or until potatoes are fork-tender and top is golden brown.

4. Let stand 10–15 minutes before serving.

# Homemade Green Bean Casserole

**Prep time: 30 min**
**Bake time: 25 min**
**Yield: 8 servings**

*I laughed at the Pea Comic where a farmer is confronted by his wife who scolds: "You just had to put in fifteen hundred acres of corn when you know darn well all my casseroles call for green beans." Well, lucky for me, I have green beans and, yes, I make a green bean casserole each Thanksgiving. However, this isn't your ordinary green bean casserole! It has crispy shallots and a creamy, cheesy homemade base. And you know that everything tastes better with cheese!*

## INGREDIENTS

1½ pounds green beans, trimmed

3 ounces bacon, cooked and chopped (reserve grease)

1½ pounds mushrooms, sliced

4 cloves garlic, minced or pressed

½ teaspoon crushed dried thyme

½ teaspoon salt

½ teaspoon ground black pepper

### SAUCE

2 tablespoons butter

2 tablespoons flour

1½ cups half-and-half

1 (5.2-ounce) package semisoft cheese with garlic and fine herbs, broken into pieces (for example, Boursin brand)

⅛ teaspoon salt

⅛ teaspoon ground black pepper

¼ cup white cooking wine

1 recipe Crispy Shallots or 1 cup canned French-fried onions (optional)

### CRISPY SHALLOTS (OPTIONAL)

¾ cup vegetable oil

4 large shallots or 1 large sweet onion, thinly sliced (about 1 cup)

½ cup milk

1 cup flour

## INSTRUCTIONS

1. Preheat oven to 375 degrees F. Grease a 2- or 3-quart baking dish; set aside.

2. In a large saucepan over medium-high heat, cook beans in enough water to cover the beans for 3 to 5 minutes or until crisp tender; drain. Transfer to a large bowl of ice water to stop cooking. Drain again. Set aside.

3. In a large skillet, add mushrooms, garlic, and thyme to grease drippings from bacon (or, if you prefer, 2 tablespoons olive oil) and cook over medium heat until mushrooms are tender and liquid evaporated (about 5 minutes). Stir in bacon, salt, and pepper. Add mushroom mixture to green beans and toss.

4. Gently fold in sauce to green bean mixture until well combined. Transfer to prepared baking dish. Bake for 25–30 minutes or until bubbly and beans are tender.

5. If using, top with French-fried onions the last 5 minutes of baking. Let stand 10 minutes before serving. Sprinkle with optional crispy shallots.

## SAUCE

1. Melt butter in a small saucepan over medium heat. Stir in flour, cook, and stir for 1 minute. Add half-and-half. Continue cooking and stirring over medium heat until thick and bubbly. Whisk in semisoft cheese, salt, and pepper. Remove from heat and stir in cooking wine.

## CRISPY SHALLOTS

1. In a small saucepan over medium-high heat, warm oil. Dip shallots in milk, allowing excess to drip off. Dredge in flour and place in hot oil. Cook about 1 to 2 minutes or until golden and slightly crisp. Remove with a slotted spoon and transfer to a plate lined with paper towels to drain. Lightly sprinkle with salt. Repeat as needed with remaining shallots.

# Festive Pumpkin-Shaped Rolls

Bake time: 15–20 min
Yield: 24 rolls

*Thanksgiving can get incredibly busy, and so sometimes I like to take the easy route and use premade dough for rolls. You must try these rolls at least once. They are so festive and easy, and they always get rave reviews. You can make these with premade dough or use your favorite roll recipe!*

## INGREDIENTS

1 large (36-count) package frozen Rhodes Rolls (or use one of your favorite premade dough or roll recipes)

1 egg + 1 teaspoon water, beaten

1 tablespoon butter, melted

# INSTRUCTIONS

1. If you are using Rhodes Rolls or another frozen variety, thaw per package instructions. Alternately, put several frozen rolls on a microwave-safe plate and thaw in the microwave for 1 minute, turn over, and microwave for 30 seconds to 1 minute more. The dough will defrost and come out soft and malleable. NOTE: Do NOT overcook or they'll turn hard and be unusable.

2. Form together 1½ balls of dough into one. Or, if using your own recipe, form a 1½- to 2-inch round ball of dough.

3. Line two baking sheets with parchment paper and set aside.

4. Turn the dough ball onto a lightly floured surface. Press down on the dough with your hand to slightly flatten it.

5. Using a paring knife, slice 8 segments around the dough, leaving the center uncut. It will end up looking like a flower. Place the dough on the prepared baking sheet. Using your finger, poke a hole in the center of the dough. Your "pumpkin" is starting to take shape! Repeat the process on unshaped dough.

6. Cover the rolls and let rise in a warm place until double in size (30 minutes to 1 hour). After the rolls rise, you may notice that the indentation in the center of the roll has disappeared. Just gently re-poke a hole in the center with your finger.

7. Gently brush the beaten egg wash onto each roll.

8. Bake at 325 degrees F for 15–20 minutes or until golden brown. Remove and brush each roll with melted butter to give them a shine.

9. Insert a pecan half into the center hole, which now becomes your stem! Cute, huh?

# Funeral Potatoes

**Prep time:** 20 min
**Bake time:** 50 min
**Yield:** 12 servings

*Funeral Potatoes are a cheesy potato casserole that receive their tongue-in-cheek
name by always being part of a luncheon after a Latter-day Saint\* funeral. Despite
its sad name, it's anything but! It's pretty much impossible to dislike this potato dish bathed
in melted cheese, sour cream, onions, and garlic, and layered with a crunchy top. Divine.*

## INGREDIENTS

6 tablespoons butter

¾ cup onion, diced

2 cloves garlic, minced

One 30-ounce bag of frozen, shredded
hashbrown potatoes, thawed (or 12 small
potatoes parboiled and shredded)

One (10.5-ounce) can condensed cream of
chicken soup

1 cup sour cream or plain Greek yogurt

¼ cup grated Parmesan cheese

1 teaspoon salt

½ teaspoon ground black pepper

2 cups sharp cheddar cheese, shredded and
firmly packed

1½ cups crushed cornflake cereal or panko
bread crumbs

## INSTRUCTIONS

1. Preheat oven to 350 degrees F.

2. In a medium skillet, sauté onions in 2 tablespoons butter until onions are soft and translucent. Stir in the
   garlic and cook until fragrant. Remove from heat and set aside.

3. In a large bowl, mix together the cooked onions and garlic, hashbrowns, condensed soup, sour cream or
   Greek yogurt, Parmesan cheese, salt, pepper, and 1½ cups cheddar cheese.

4. Spread the potato mixture into a 9 x 13–inch baking pan.

5. Top the casserole with the remaining ½ cup cheese.

6. Melt the remaining 4 tablespoons butter and toss with cornflakes. Sprinkle cornflakes mixture evenly over
   the top of the casserole.

7. Bake for 50–60 minutes or until heated through and bubbly.

\* *Latter-day Saint is a shortened name referencing The Church of Jesus Christ of Latter-day Saints,
most notably known as "Mormons."*

# Spinach Salad with Balsamic Strawberries and Feta Cheese

Prep time: 10 min
Cook time: none
Yield: 4 servings

*Do any of you remember the Popeye cartoons or am I just dating myself? Popeye had a fascination with spinach and he always said at the end: "I'm strong to the finich, 'cause I eats me spinach." With this salad, you'll get plenty of spinach to make you strong to the "finich."*

## INGREDIENTS

### VINAIGRETTE

½ cup extra virgin olive oil

¼ cup balsamic vinegar

2 tablespoons agave (or 3 tablespoons honey)

1½ cups whipping cream

### SALAD

6 cups fresh baby spinach

12 ounces fresh strawberries, stemmed and sliced

½ cup fresh crumbled feta cheese

½ cup chopped pecans or walnuts

salt and pepper to taste

## INSTRUCTIONS

### VINAIGRETTE

1. In a small bowl, whisk together all ingredients; set aside.

### SALAD

1. In a large mixing bowl, add spinach. Drizzle with vinaigrette and lightly toss.

2. Place on individual plates and garnish with strawberries, cheese, and nuts. Salt and pepper to taste.

# Honey Lemon Squash

**Prep time:** 10 min
**Bake time:** 50 min
**Yield:** 12 servings

*I wasn't much of a squash fan until about a year ago. I think a lot of it has to do with the way squash is cooked. One thing I rarely make for Thanksgiving (like once every 10 years) is a sweet potato casserole. If I do make the traditional casserole, my family leaves it mostly untouched. However, we are fans of this lemon maple butternut squash! It has just the right amount of buttery sweetness to endear itself to you. This is what you need to make and take to your next Thanksgiving dinner.*

## INGREDIENTS

4 pounds butternut squash, quartered and seeded

⅓ cup pure honey

⅓ cup water

zest of 1 lemon

juice of 1 lemon

butter

salt and pepper to taste (optional)

## INSTRUCTIONS

1. Preheat oven to 350 degrees F. Place squash cut-side up in a baking dish.

2. Whisk together maple syrup, water, lemon zest, and lemon juice and spoon evenly over squash.

3. Place a small amount of butter in the "bowl" of the squash. Bake for 20 minutes basting occasionally. Flip the squash one-fourth of the way and bake for 15 minutes basting halfway through. Flip one-quarter of the way to the other side and continue baking 15 minutes more, basting halfway through. Turn over and insert a fork in the center of the squash. If tender, remove. If not, continue baking until tender. Salt and pepper to taste.

4. Remove, cut into thirds, and serve warm.

# Sweet Endings

# Disney's Caramel Apple Pie (Copycat)

Prep time: 20 min
Bake time: 1 hour
Yield: 8 servings

*Several years ago we went to Disneyland. It has been on my husband's bucket list of things to do because he had NEVER been. That's pretty much blasphemous, to be in your 50s and NEVER have been to Disneyland, don't you think? We had a great time. It was everything my husband thought it would be and more. We went there in the fall, and Disneyland went full out on Halloween decorations that were simply amazing! We returned home with fantastic memories and a smattering of food to try and replicate, like this Disney Caramel Apple Pie!*

## INGREDIENTS

### CRUST

½ cup flour

16.5-ounce package of refrigerated sugar cookie dough

### FILLING

2½ pounds Granny Smith apples (4–5 apples); peeled, cored, and sliced into ½-inch pieces

½ cup sugar

⅛ cup flour

1 teaspoon Apple Pie spice

½ cup bottled caramel topping

### TOPPING

1 cup flour

½ cup granulated sugar

½ cup packed brown sugar

1 teaspoon Apple Pie spice

1 teaspoon pure vanilla extract

6 tablespoons cold butter, chopped

## INSTRUCTIONS

1. Preheat oven to 350 degrees F. Coat a 9-inch springform cake pan with cooking spray; set aside.

2. Add flour and refrigerated cookie dough to a large mixing bowl. Using a pastry knife, cut in the cookie dough and flour until pea-size pieces form. Shape dough into a large disc and transfer to prepared springform pan. Firmly press and work dough against the bottom and sides of pan to form a ¼-inch thick crust; set aside.

3. In a large mixing bowl, toss together apples, sugar, flour, and spice until well coated; transfer to prepared crust. Drizzle caramel topping across the top of apple mixture. Cover with foil and bake for 45 minutes.

4. Meanwhile, combine flour, sugars, spice, and extract in a medium bowl. Cut in butter until mixture resembles coarse crumbs. Remove foil from pie and sprinkle topping over baked pie. Leave uncovered and continue baking 15 to 20 minutes or until topping is lightly browned.

5. Remove from oven and allow to cool on a wire rack. Remove sides of springform pan when ready to serve. Garnish with additional caramel topping, if desired.

# Easy Pumpkin Seed Brittle

Yield: 1¾ pounds brittle or 28 servings

*"Let the word go forth that today the torch has been passed to a new generation of [pumpkin growers]" (President John F. Kennedy's Inaugural Address, January 20, 1961). I'm passing the torch on to you, my friends… dig out those pumpkin seeds, toast them, and make them into tasty pumpkin seed brittle. A fun twist to the original peanut brittle.*

## INGREDIENTS

¼ cup salted butter

½ cup packed light-brown sugar

¼ cup honey

1 cup hulled pumpkin seeds

1 teaspoon pure vanilla extract

1 teaspoon cinnamon

## INSTRUCTIONS

1. Prepare a 10 x 15–inch baking sheet with a coating of cooking spray; set aside.

2. In a small saucepan over medium heat, melt butter. Stir in sugar and honey and bring to a boil. Cook, without stirring, until a candy thermometer registers 280 degrees. Immediately stir in vanilla, cinnamon, and pumpkin seeds and continue cooking until thermometer registers 300 degrees.

3. Pour into prepared baking sheet and use a spatula to evenly spread and fill pan. Let cool completely before breaking into pieces (about 30 to 40 minutes)

# Chocolate Peanut Butter Dessert

Prep time: 20 min
Bake time: 10 min
+ 3 hours to chill

*There's just something about chocolate that is comforting. It doesn't ask stupid questions; it just simply understands. I haven't encountered a problem yet that can't be solved with chocolate. For example…Need to exercise? Try Nestlé crunches. Need comfort? Try this chocolate peanut butter dessert.*

## INGREDIENTS

### CHOCOLATE CRUST

1¼ cups white granulated sugar

⅔ cup flour

¾ cup unsweetened cocoa powder

1 pinch salt

½ cup butter, melted

### FILLING

8 ounces cream cheese, softened

½ cup peanut butter

1½ cups powdered sugar, divided

16 ounces frozen whipped topping, thawed, divided

15–20 miniature peanut butter cups, chopped

1 cup cold milk

3.9 ounces instant chocolate pudding mix

crushed Oreos (optional)

## INSTRUCTIONS

### CHOCOLATE CRUST

1. Preheat oven to 325 degrees F.

2. In a medium-sized bowl, stir together sugar, flour, cocoa powder, and salt. Add melted butter and stir until well blended.

3. Press dough into the bottom and up the sides of a 9-inch pie pan. Bake for about 10 minutes or until sides are firm but not hard.

### FILLING

1. Beat together cream cheese, peanut butter, and 1 cup powdered sugar until smooth and creamy. Fold in half of the whipped topping until well combined. Spread over pie crust. Sprinkle with chopped peanut butter cups.

2. In a separate bowl with electric beaters, whip together milk, pudding mix, and remaining powdered sugar on low speed for 2 minutes. Let stand until soft set. Fold in remaining whipped topping and spread over top of peanut butter cups. Sprinkle with crushed Oreos, if desired. Cover and chill for 3 hours or overnight.

# Pumpkin Spice Cupcakes with Maple Cream Cheese Frosting

Prep time: 10 min
Bake time: 20 min
Yield: 12 cupcakes

*In the days that followed Thanksgiving, I made these pumpkin spice cupcakes topped with maple cream cheese frosting. This was the most popular breakfast, lunch, dinner, and snack. They may have been gone in two days. I may not have shared. I may have hidden them in my closet. I may...*

## INGREDIENTS

1 cup flour

1 teaspoon baking powder

½ teaspoon baking soda

½ teaspoon salt

1 teaspoon ground cinnamon

½ teaspoon ground ginger

2 large eggs, beaten

1 cup canned pumpkin purée (not pumpkin pie purée)

½ cup granulated sugar

½ cup brown sugar, lightly packed

½ cup vegetable oil

### MAPLE CREAM CHEESE FROSTING

8-ounce block cream cheese, at room temperature

1 cup unsalted butter, at room temperature

2 tablespoons real maple syrup

1 pound powdered sugar

## INSTRUCTIONS

1. Preheat oven to 350 degrees F. Prepare muffin tin with 12 liners; set aside.

2. In a medium mixing bowl, sift together flour, baking powder, baking soda, salt, cinnamon, and ginger; set aside.

3. In a large mixing bowl, whisk together eggs, pumpkin, sugars, and oil. Add flour mixture and stir until well combined.

4. Divide batter into muffin tins filling about ⅔ or ¾ full. Bake in preheated oven for 20 minutes or until a toothpick entered into the center of a cupcake comes out clean. Remove from oven and let cool completely before removing. Frost with maple cream cheese frosting.

# Aunt Eloise's Secret for Stabalized Whipping Cream

**Prep time: 30 min**
**Yield: varies**

*All families have some kind of dirty little secret lurking in their closets. I mean, my family has lots of them! How do you think we put "fun" in dysfunctional? So I thought I would share with you one dirty little secret in my family and that's how to thicken whipping cream and make it last for days. One day, my great aunt Eloise (who's now in her 90s!) was in town, and I saw her put this strange thick white glob in the cream she was whipping. "What was that you just put in the whipping cream?" I asked inquisitively. She answered matter-of-factly: "Cream cheese." Now why would she put cream cheese in whipping cream? Maybe she just loves cheese like I do and can't make anything without cheese. But still, I had to ask—"Why do you put cream cheese in whipping cream?" She informed me that the cream cheese thickens up the whipping cream AND sets it so it will last for days. Can I just tell you how excited I was? It was like Ben Franklin discovering electricity! So I went home and tried it and guess what? It works! I've been using cream cheese in my whipping cream since, and now it's some twenty-plus years later.*

## INGREDIENTS

Heavy whipping cream, any size

(NOTE: *the amount of butterfat contained in whipping cream determines how well the cream will whip and how stable it will be. Heavy whipping cream also doubles in volume when whipped. So you get more bang for your buck! Use 1 cup of cream to make 2 cups of whipped cream*)

1–2 tablespoons of superfine sugar or other sugar substitute per 1 cup of cream

1 heaping teaspoon cream cheese per 1 cup of cream

## INSTRUCTIONS

1. Whipping cream works much better if you chill your bowl and beaters in the fridge for approximately 15 minutes before whipping. Remove from fridge.

2. Pour the cream in a large enough bowl that the cream won't splatter while whipping and which accommodates twice the amount of cream, since after it is whipped it will double in size.

3. With an electric mixer, beat cream for 20–30 seconds on low until bubbles begin to form.

4. Increase mixer speed to medium and beat until the cream begins to thicken and form a soft peak. Add sugar a little at a time to your heart's content.

5. Now here's the secret: Increase the mixer speed to high and slowly add 1 heaping teaspoon cream cheese per 1 cup cream. Beat until the cream begins to thicken and forms a stiff peak. NOTE: *Be sure to move the beaters along the sides and bottom of the bowl while whipping the cream.*

6. For a soft peak, beat until a soft peak forms when pulling the beaters straight up out of the mixture.

7. For a stiff peak, continue beating at high speed. You will know when the cream is done when you pull out the beaters and it sticks to the beaters.

8. Store in an airtight container in the coldest part of the fridge up to a week or 10 days.

NOTE: *Whipped cream is generally sweetened with sugar. The whipped cream can be sweetened with granulated sugar, superfine sugar, or powdered sugar. Superfine and powdered sugars dissolve quicker and won't be as gritty. Powdered sugar also helps stabilize whipping cream because it contains cornstarch.*

# Bloomin' Baked Apple with Caramel Sauce

Prep time: 15 min
Bake time: 25–45 min
Yield: 4 servings

*Have you ever tried onion blossoms at restaurants? They're like an onion and a flower in one. Masterful. Have you ever tried baked apple blossoms? They're like an apple and a flower in one but with a heck of a better flavor. Genius.*

## INGREDIENTS

2 Honeycrisp or Gala apples

4 individually wrapped caramels, unwrapped

4 tablespoons butter

3 tablespoons packed brown sugar

1 tablespoon flour

pinch of salt

1 teaspoon apple pie spice

ice cream and caramel sauce (optional)

# INSTRUCTIONS

1. Preheat oven to 375 degrees F.

2. Turn apple sideways and slice off the top third of the apple. Discard top.

3. Using a melon baller or metal teaspoon measuring spoon, scoop out the core.

4. With a thin knife, cut in two deep circular cuts around the center of the apple. Cut down deep enough but not all the way through.

5. Turn the apple upside down and, from about ¼ of an inch from the center, make narrow vertical slits all the way around the apple, making sure to cut down clear through.

6. Turn the apple right-side up and place in an oven-safe dish. Place two caramels in the center of each apple.

7. Place butter and brown sugar in a microwave-safe bowl and melt in the microwave for 30 seconds on high; stir and microwave 30 seconds longer. Remove from microwave and stir in flour, salt, and apple pie spice. Evenly divide mixture over the top of apples.

8. Depending on the size of apples, bake for 25–45 minutes or until the apples are soft and tender. Using a large spoon, transfer apples to a bowl. If your apples don't fall open, use two forks to spread apart. Top with ice cream and caramel sauce if desired. Serve while warm.

# Pumpkin Pecan Pie

Prep time: 20 min
Bake time: 1 hour
+ 2 hours for cooling

*My family really loved this pie—pumpkin pie and pecan pie all in one! Why not make one pie instead of two to satisfy everyone's cravings? Genius! You'll adore this recipe.*

## INGREDIENTS

15 ounces pumpkin purée

2 eggs, beaten

½ cup half-and-half

¾ cup white sugar

1 tablespoon flour

1 teaspoon lemon zest

½ teaspoon vanilla extract

¼ teaspoon salt

1 teaspoon pumpkin pie spice

¼ teaspoon ground cinnamon

1 (9-inch) prepared pie shell

¾ cup packed dark brown sugar

1 cup chopped pecans

½ teaspoon ground cinnamon

3 tablespoons butter, softened (not melted)

## INSTRUCTIONS

1. Preheat oven to 425 degrees F.

2. Beat together pumpkin purée, egg, and half-and-half until smooth and creamy.

3. Stir in sugar, flour, lemon zest, vanilla, salt, pumpkin pie spice, and cinnamon until well incorporated. Pour into prepared pie shell. Cover edges with foil, to prevent burning, and bake for 15 minutes; reduce heat to 350 degrees F and bake 20 minutes more.

4. Meanwhile, stir together brown sugar, pecans, and cinnamon. Work in butter until mixture is well combined. While pie is still in oven, carefully spoon pecan mixture to top of pie. Continue cooking for 20–25 minutes more or until a knife inserted in the center of the pie comes out clean.

5. Cool on a wire rack for 2 hours or more before serving.

# Old-Fashioned Sweet Potato Pie

Prep time: 20 min
Bake time: 45 min
Yield: 6–8 servings

*I was recently in Cincinnati with other bloggers at a cooking event for a retailer. They gave us three ingredients and we had to cook up a recipe or recipes with what was given us. We could buy more ingredients if we wanted, but we had to use all three that we were given. My ingredients were salmon, sweet potatoes, and blueberries. I chose to do a sweet potato pie with my sweet potatoes! While it was baking, the smell drove me crazy! It smelled like a piece of heaven. When it came time to taste test our dishes, I am happy to say this pie was completely eaten and raved about for all three days we were there!*

## INGREDIENTS

### PIE FILLING

2 cups peeled, baked, and puréed sweet potatoes (do not boil sweet potatoes; it makes them too moist)

1 cup sugar

¼ cup melted butter

4 large eggs

1 teaspoon pure vanilla extract

¼ teaspoon salt

¼ teaspoon ground cloves

1 teaspoon ground cinnamon

½ teaspoon ground ginger

1 cup almond milk

1 unbaked 9-inch deep-dish pie shell

### MERINGUE

3 egg whites

¼ cup granulated sugar

## INSTRUCTIONS

### FILLING

1. Preheat oven to 350 degrees F.
2. Combine puréed potatoes, sugar, butter, eggs, vanilla, salt, and spices and mix with an electric mixer until smooth.
3. Slowly add milk and continue beating until blended (filling will be thin).
4. Pour filling into unbaked pie shell and bake for 35 to 45 minutes or until a knife inserted in the center comes out clean.
5. Transfer to a wire rack to cool to room temperature before topping with meringue.

## MERINGUE

1. Using an electric mixer, beat egg whites on high until soft peaks form. Continue beating adding sugar a little at a time until sugar dissolves and stiff peaks form.

2. Using a rubber spatula, spread meringue on the pie swirling peaks around the pie as you go and making sure the meringue touches the edge all around.

3. Bake for 10 to 12 minutes or until lightly browned.

4. Transfer to a wire rack to cool completely before serving.

# Thanksgiving Leftovers

# Creamy Turkey Pot Pie Soup with Parmesan Biscuits

**Prep time: 30 min**
**Bake time: 45 min**

## INGREDIENTS

### SOUP

10 ounces turkey meat, cooked and chopped into bite-size pieces

5½ tablespoons butter, divided

1 small yellow onion, chopped

3 stalks celery, diced

2 carrots, chopped

32 ounces low-sodium vegetable broth

2 medium russet potatoes peeled and cubed

½ teaspoon dried parsley

¼ teaspoon dried thyme

¼ teaspoon dried rosemary

1 bay leaf

salt and ground black pepper to taste

1 cup peas

2½ cups milk

4 tablespoons flour

½ cup heavy cream

1 recipe for Garlic-Parmesan Drop Biscuits (recipe follows)

### BISCUITS

1½ cups flour

1½ teaspoons baking powder

½ teaspoon salt

⅛ teaspoon ground black pepper

¼ teaspoon garlic powder

6 tablespoons unsalted butter, chopped

½ cup finely shredded Parmesan cheese

½ cup milk

¼ cup heavy cream

## INSTRUCTIONS

### SOUP

1. In a large stockpot, melt 1½ tablespoons butter over medium-high heat. Add onion, carrots, and celery. Sauté until onions are transparent. Add vegetable broth, potatoes, parsley, thyme, rosemary, and bay leaf and season with salt and pepper to taste. Bring to a boil, stir, reduce heat to medium, cover with lid, and cook until potatoes are tender (about 15–20 minutes). Reduce heat to low, remove bay leaf, and stir in turkey and peas.

2. Meanwhile, melt remaining 4 tablespoons butter in a medium saucepan over medium heat. Stir in flour and continuously stir until well combined. Slowly pour milk into mixture while whisking vigorously to

smooth out lumps. Increase temperature to medium-high and bring to a boil, stirring constantly. Remove from heat and stir in cream. Pour mixture into stock and mix well.

3. Top with Garlic-Parmesan Drop Biscuits and serve.

## BISCUITS

1. Preheat oven to 450 degrees F. Line a baking sheet with parchment paper; set aside.

2. In a large bowl, mix together flour, baking powder, salt, pepper, and garlic powder until well incorporated.

3. Add butter and, with a pastry cutter or fork, cut butter into flour mixture. Continue until mixture resembles coarse crumbs.

4. Pour in milk and heavy cream and stir until well combined. (Batter will be sticky and lumpy.)

5. Drop about ¼ cup batter onto prepared baking sheet. Cook for 10 minutes or until golden brown. Remove and let cool before serving.

# Leftover Turkey Stuffing Croquettes

Prep time: 15 min
Bake time: 20 min
Yield: 12 servings

*Waste not, want not. If we don't waste what we have, we'll still have it in the future and will not lack it. This is my version of using up Thanksgiving leftovers and wasting not. The recipe is ridiculously simple and combines everything you should have on hand from the dinner you made the day before.*

## INGREDIENTS

4 tablespoons butter, divided

1 small yellow onion, finely chopped

1 teaspoon of your favorite all-seasoning (I like Morton Nature's Seasons Seasoning Blend)

½ cup heavy cream

1 teaspoon lemon juice

2 cups finely chopped cooked turkey

1 cup prepared stuffing

1 large beaten egg, divided

2 cups bread crumbs

turkey gravy for serving

## INSTRUCTIONS

1. In a medium skillet over medium heat, melt 3 tablespoons butter, add onions, and sauté until transparent. Whisk in seasoning, cream, and lemon juice. Remove from heat; set aside, and cool about 15 minutes.

2. Meanwhile, line baking sheet with foil or a silicon mat and add remaining tablespoon of butter. Place in oven to melt. Remove and use a brush to spread the butter over the pan evenly.

3. In a large mixing bowl, add ½ egg to stuffing and mix well. Add turkey and onion mixture. Stir well until well combined. Place breadcrumbs in a small mixing bowl. Form stuffing mixture into 12 egg-shaped balls. Roll eggs in remaining egg mixture, transfer to breadcrumbs, and spoon crumbs over balls until completely covered. Transfer to baking sheet. Repeat with remaining balls.

4. Bake in preheated oven for 20–30 minutes until browned. Remove and serve warm with turkey gravy.

Prep time: 15 min
Bake time: 5 min
Yield: 4 servings

# Turkey Cobb Scramble

*One thing I am known for is my scrambled eggs. Somewhere down the line of making really soggy eggs and extremely dry eggs, I finally mastered a flawless scramble. Scrambled eggs are the perfect canvas for any filling, like this turkey cobb. All the ingredients in a cobb salad are made into scrambled eggs (minus the lettuce, of course).*

## INGREDIENTS

6 eggs, beaten

¼ cup milk

1 avocado, pitted, peeled, and chopped

½ cup chopped turkey

2 heaping tablespoons real bacon pieces

¼ cup crumbled blue cheese

¼ cup chopped green onions

1 Roma tomato, seeded and chopped

salt and pepper to taste

## INSTRUCTIONS

1. Lightly coat a nonstick skillet with cooking spray and warm up over medium-high heat.

2. Whisk together eggs and milk until well combined. Fold in remaining ingredients and pour into warmed skillet. Stir occasionally until eggs are set but still moist.

Prep time: 10 min
Cook time: 2 min
Yield: 4 sandwiches

# Turkey Caprese Sandwich

*I just love the word caprese [kuh-prey-zee]. It's a fun word to say that just rolls off your tongue and makes you sound very Italian! Caprese is prepared with fresh mozzarella, tomatoes, basil, and olive oil...all of the ingredients used to make this turkey caprese sandwich.*

## INGREDIENTS

8 slices of bread of choice, such as brioche or challah

½ cup mayonnaise

¼ cup basil pesto

14 ounces shredded turkey

12 sundried tomatoes

4 slices mozzarella cheese

2 tablespoons extra virgin olive oil

## INSTRUCTIONS

1. Mix together mayo and pesto and spread half of mixture on 4 slices of bread. Top with turkey, sundried tomatoes, and mozzarella.

2. Turn oven on broil. Brush olive oil on the other 4 slices of bread and arrange on a baking sheet. Broil for 1 to 2 minutes or until bread is lightly browned. (If desired, broil the other half of the sandwich to melt the cheese.) Remove from oven, top with remaining pesto, and serve while hot.

# Turkey Corn Chowder

Prep time: 15 min
Bake time: 5 min
Yield: 4 servings

## INGREDIENTS

1½ tablespoons olive oil

all-seasoning or salt and pepper to taste

8 slices bacon, diced

1 yellow onion, peeled and diced

3 sticks celery, diced

½ jalapeño pepper, stemmed, seeded, and diced

1½ tablespoons dried oregano seasoning

½ teaspoon ground sage

1 cup white cooking wine

1 (26-ounce) can chicken stock

1 cup frozen super sweet corn, thawed

1 pound turkey, cooked and diced into bite-sized pieces

2 cups whipping cream

## INSTRUCTIONS

1. In a large stockpot, warm up oil over medium heat. Add bacon, onion, celery, jalapeño, oregano, and sage. Sauté until bacon is cooked through and vegetables are tender.

2. Add cooking wine and continue cooking until reduced in half; stirring occasionally to make sure vegetables do not burn. Add chicken stock, corn, and turkey. Bring to a boil.

3. Add milk and half-and-half and bring back to a boil. Cover and reduce heat to medium low and allow to simmer for an hour, stirring occasionally.

4. Remove lid and continue simmering for an additional 15 minutes, stirring occasionally. If needed, salt and pepper to taste.

# CHRISTMAS MENU

# Blitzen Breakfast and Brunch

# Breakfast Enchiladas

Prep time: 20 min
Bake time: 30 min

*Sometimes the things kids say can be, well, embarrassing! Like the time when we were on the beach and our oldest son was wearing a Speedo. My 6-year-old nephew inquisitively said, "Taco, burrito, what's in your Speedo?" Ha-ha. Just a classic. Whenever I make Mexican-type food, my mind drifts back to that distant memory and it always makes me laugh.*

*These breakfast enchiladas are definitely a once-in-a-while-when-calories-don't-count meal. It is enough to feed every hungry heart.*

## INGREDIENTS

### CHEESE SAUCE

⅓ cup butter

⅓ cup flour

3 cups milk

2 (8-ounce) cups shredded Monterey Jack cheese

1 (4.5-ounce) can chopped green chiles, undrained and divided

¾ teaspoon salt

### ENCHILADAS

1 pound spicy ground pork sausage

12 large eggs, beaten

¼ cup milk

4 green onions, thinly sliced

2 tablespoons chopped fresh cilantro

2 tomatoes, seeded and chopped, divided

remaining chopped green chiles, drained

¾ teaspoon salt

½ teaspoon pepper

2 tablespoons butter

cheese sauce (recipe to follow)

8 (8-inch) flour tortillas

1 cup Monterey Jack cheese

garnish with tomatoes, green onion, and fresh cilantro

## INSTRUCTIONS

### CHEESE SAUCE

1.  Melt butter in a large saucepan over medium-low heat; whisk in flour and continue stirring while cooking for one minute. Increase heat to medium and gradually whisk in milk, stirring constantly for 5 minutes or until thickened. Remove from heat and stir in cheese, half of chiles, and salt.

## ENCHILADAS

1. Preheat oven to 350 degrees F. Prepare a 9 × 13–inch baking dish with cooking spray; set aside.

2. Crumble sausage in a large skillet. Cook over medium-high heat, stirring often until meat is no longer pink. Remove from pan. Set aside.

3. In a large bowl, whisk together eggs and milk until well combined. Whisk in green onion, cilantro, half of tomatoes, remaining chopped green chiles, salt, and pepper.

4. Return skillet to stove and melt butter over medium heat. Pour egg mixture in skillet and cook without stirring until eggs begin to set on bottom. Draw a spatula across bottom of pan to form large curds. Continue to cook and draw spatula across bottom of pan until eggs are thickened and cooked through but still moist. Remove from heat and fold in 1½ cups cheese sauce and sausage.

5. Spoon about ⅓ cup egg mixture down the center of a flour tortilla, roll up, and place seam-side down in prepared baking dish. Repeat for remaining tortillas. Pour remaining cheese sauce evenly over top of rolled tortillas. Sprinkle with 1 cup Monterey Jack cheese and remaining tomatoes.

6. Bake for 30 minutes or until bubbly. Serve while warm.

# Overnight Blueberry French Toast

Prep time: 15 min
Bake time: 55 min
Yield: 10–12 servings

*Here's a little trivia for you: French toast really wasn't invented in France. It can actually be traced back to the Roman Empire in a cookbook attributed to Apicius. The word "French toast" was later coined in England, which was brought to America by early settlers, and popularized by French immigrants.*

## INGREDIENTS

### FRENCH TOAST

10–12 slices of Texas Toast or thickly sliced bread, cut into 1-inch cubes, divided

2 (8-ounce) blocks cream cheese, cubed

2 cups fresh blueberries, divided

12 eggs, beaten

2 cups milk

1 teaspoon vanilla extract

⅓ cup pure maple syrup

1 teaspoon cinnamon

½ teaspoon nutmeg

### TOPPING

1 cup granulated sugar

2 tablespoons cornstarch

1 cup water

⅛ teaspoon cinnamon

1 tablespoon butter

## INSTRUCTIONS

1. Prepare 9 × 13–inch baking dish with a light coating of cooking spray. Line the bottom of the baking dish with half of the bread cubes. Layer with cream cheese cubes and blueberries. Top with remaining bread cubes; set aside.

2. In a large mixing bowl, whisk together eggs, milk, vanilla, syrup, cinnamon and nutmeg. Pour evenly over the bread mixture making sure to coat all of the bread with egg mixture. Cover tightly with foil and refrigerate overnight.

3. In the morning, preheat oven to 350 degrees Fahrenheit. Keep dish covered with foil and bake for 30 minutes. Uncover and continue baking for 20–25 minutes or until center is firm to the touch.

4. Meanwhile, in a medium sauce pan stir together sugar, cornstarch and water and bring to a boil; stirring constantly. Reduce heat and stir in remaining cup of blueberries and simmer for approximately 10 minutes stirring occasionally. Stir in butter until melted and pour mixture of baked French toast. Serve while warm.

# Make-Ahead Cinnamon Rolls with Cream Cheese Frosting

Prep time: 25 min
+ rising time
Bake time: 12 min
Yield: 12 rolls

*These are my infamous cinnamon rolls. When we had new hire meetings at my job, I was in charge of ordering the food for the week-long event. On the last day of one of the trainings, I brought in these cinnamon rolls. From there on out, it was the most requested item and always got scarfed down.*

## INGREDIENTS

### ROLLS

1 package yeast (¼ ounce or 2¼ teaspoons)

2 tablespoons warm water

1 cup hot water

1 teaspoon salt

⅓ cup shortening, melted

¼ cup sugar

1 egg, beaten

3½ cups flour

### FILLING

¾ cup brown sugar, firmly packed

¼ cup flour

1 tablespoon ground cinnamon

½ cup butter, melted

½ cup raisins (optional)

### CREAM CHEESE FROSTING

8 ounces cream cheese, softened

1 cup butter, softened

2 pounds powdered sugar

2 teaspoons pure vanilla extract

## INSTRUCTIONS

### ROLLS

1. Dissolve yeast in 2 tablespoons warm water (100–110 F). Let stand to activate and foam (about 10 minutes). If mixture is foamy, yeast is active.

2. In a large bowl, whisk together 1 cup hot water, salt, shortening and sugar. Add yeast mixture, egg, and flour. Stir until well combined. Cover with plastic wrap and a kitchen towel and place in refrigerator overnight (it will rise overnight).

3. Remove from refrigerator and knead dough for approximately 5 minutes until soft, elastic, and warmed to room temperature.

4. Turn onto a lightly floured work surface. With a rolling pin, roll dough into a rectangle of approximately 18 × 12 inches.

5. For filling: Combine brown sugar, flour, and cinnamon. With a spoon, spread the butter out evenly across the dough surface. Generously sprinkle cinnamon/sugar mixture evenly over rolled-out dough. Sprinkle raisins throughout, if desired.

6. Starting from the long side, tightly roll up dough into a spiral log. Firmly pinch seam to seal. Cut log into twelve 1½-inch wide slices. An easy way to do this is to score the log with a sharp knife to mark 12 rolls. Using dental floss, slide the floss under the roll at the score mark. Cross the floss over the top of the dough, pull tightly until it cuts through. You'll get a nice, sharp cut.

7. Lightly grease a 13 × 9 × 2–inch baking pan. Arrange slices onto the prepared pan. Cover with a towel and let rise in a warm place until nearly double in size (about 45 minutes).

8. Preheat oven to 375 degrees F. Bake uncovered for 12–15 minutes or until lightly golden brown. Remove from oven and cool in pan on a wire rack for 5 minutes. Spread with cream cheese frosting.

## CREAM CHEESE FROSTING

1. With an electric mixer on medium speed, beat together cream cheese until creamy. Reduce speed to low and gradually add sugar until smooth and creamy. Add vanilla and continue beating until well blended.

# Mom's Homemade Utah Scones

Prep time: 20 min + rising time
Bake time: 2 min
Yield: 2 dozen

*I have a secret the rest of the world is missing out on: a secret recipe for scones. I know, I know, these don't look like your "typical" scone. At least, not the way the rest of the world knows scones. I had no idea that the scones I know and love are actually* **Utah Scones***. A Utah scone is a plate-sized, golden-fried, puffy piece of greatness served up with honey butter, syrup, or powdered sugar. They're more like Navajo fry bread or Sopapillas where you use a sweet yeast dough, cut up into squares or balls of dough, deep fry them, and smother them in syrup, powdered sugar, or honey butter. Mom made these "scones" during my growing-up years. We could count on "scones" for breakfast, especially for special occasions.*

## INGREDIENTS

1 cup water, hot

1 tablespoon active dry yeast

⅓ cup oil or melted shortening

1 teaspoon salt

¼ cup sugar

3½ cups flour, sifted

1 egg, beaten

2 quarts frying oil (e.g. safflower or canola oil)

## INSTRUCTIONS

1. Mix 3 tablespoons of warm water with yeast adding a pinch of sugar. Set aside for 10 minutes for yeast to activate and foam.

2. In the meantime, combine hot water, oil (or melted shortening), salt, and sugar in a large bowl.

3. Once the yeast has activated, add egg to the yeast mixture. Mix well.

4. Add the egg/yeast mixture to the oil/sugar mixture. Stir well.

5. Gradually add flour stirring well after each addition. Knead the dough as it stiffens until you get a doughy, elastic consistency. About 5 minutes.

## MAKE AHEAD METHOD

1. Place dough in a well-greased bowl, turning once to grease the top. Cover with plastic wrap and a towel and place in the refrigerator overnight.

2. Remove from fridge and knead lightly.

3. Because the dough is still cold, cover with a towel or oil-sprayed plastic wrap and let rise until double (about 1–2 hours).

NOTE: *I like to let my dough rise in a warmed oven. I set the temperature to 170 degrees Fahrenheit and warm for approximately 1 minute. Turn oven off, place dough in oven, and let rise until double in size.*

## DAY-OF METHOD

1. Place dough in a well-greased bowl, turning once to grease the top. Let dough rise for about 30 minutes or until double in size.

## TO FRY

1. Line a plate with paper towels and set aside.

2. Fill a large sauce pan with 2 inches of oil and heat to 350–375 degrees F over medium-high heat. Once temperature is reached, reduce heat slightly.

3. Meanwhile, punch down dough and divide into 12 balls. Roll out a piece of dough on a lightly floured surface into ¼-inch thick circles or squares. You can use your fingers to stretch out the balls of dough, too. We like ours thick!

4. Carefully place two or three balls of dough in the oil with metal tongs and fry until golden brown on each side (about 1–2 minutes on each side). Remove with metal tongues. Transfer to paper towels to drain. Repeat until dough is all fried.

5. Serve hot with honey butter, butter, syrup, or powdered sugar.

# Lemon Blueberry Bread

**Prep time: 10 min**
**Cook time: 1 hour**
**Yield: 4–6 servings**

*What to do when life gives you lemons...give the lemons back. Get mad. And make lemon blueberry bread (it tastes better).*

## INGREDIENTS

### BREAD

1½ cups flour

1 teaspoon salt

1 teaspoon baking powder

⅓ cup butter, melted

¾ cup sugar

3 tablespoons lemon juice

2 eggs, beaten

½ cup unsweetened almond milk

1½ cups fresh blueberries (if frozen, make sure they are thawed)

### ICING

1 tablespoon butter, melted

1 tablespoon lemon juice

2 tablespoons grated lemon zest (optional)

1 cup powdered sugar, sifted

1 tablespoon butter

## INSTRUCTIONS

### BREAD

1. Preheat oven to 350 degrees F. Lightly grease an 8 × 4–inch bread pan and cut out parchment paper or silicon pads to fit the bottom of the pan.

2. In a small mixing bowl, mix together flour, salt and baking powder; set aside.

3. In a large mixing bowl, beat together butter, sugar, lemon juice and eggs. Alternately add flour mixture and milk to wet ingredients; mixing well after each addition.

4. Fold in blueberries. Pour into prepared loaf pan and bake for 50–60 minutes or until a toothpick entered into the center of the loaf comes out clean. Cool in pan for 10 minutes before turning out onto a wire rack. Drizzle icing on bread while still warm. Let cool completely before serving.

### ICING

1. Whisk together all ingredients into a thin icing. (If too thick, add a little almond milk to achieve the desired consistency.) Drizzle over loaf while still warm but not hot.

Prep time: 15 min
Cook time: 2 min
Yield: 8 servings

# French Toast Rollups

*Behold my favorite breakfast. It's hard to pick and choose a favorite, but these tasty rollups come to mind when people ask me. They are like miniature stuffed churros. Make them for your next brunch and listen to people gawk over them. The combination of fruit and chocolate or fruit and cheese will bowl them over.*

## INGREDIENTS

8 slices soft white sandwich bread or other soft-crusted breads

optional toppings: softened cream cheese, diced strawberries, Nutella, bananas, and/or peanut butter and jelly

2 eggs, beaten

3 tablespoons milk

⅓ cup granulated sugar

1 teaspoon ground cinnamon

butter for greasing the pan

## INSTRUCTIONS

1. Remove crust from each slice of bread with a sharp knife. Using a rolling pin, flatten out each slice.

2. Place about 1 to 2 teaspoons of chosen filling on the outer edge of bread in a strip. Roll-up each bread slice jelly roll–style. Repeat with each bread slice.

3. In a shallow bowl, whisk together eggs and milk until well combined.

4. In a separate bowl, mix together sugar and cinnamon and transfer to a plate.

5. Melt butter in a large skillet over medium heat.

6. Dip each bread roll in egg mixture, coating well. Place seam-side down in skillet and cook all sides for about 2 minutes per side until golden brown. Add butter to the pan as needed.

7. Immediately coat each cooked roll in cinnamon and sugar mixture. Serve with syrup for dipping or leave as is.

# Angelic Starters

# Christmas Layered Drink

**Prep time:** 5 min
**Cook time:** none
**Yield:** 2 servings

*Drinks can be layered with any color you'd like. The magic lies in the sugar content. The drink with the most grams of sugar content goes on the bottom, and the drink with the lightest grams goes on top. For example, the cran-apple drink has about 40 grams of sugar, the Sobe drink 25 grams, and the G2 Gatorade around 5 grams.*

## INGREDIENTS

1 cup red cran-apple juice

1 cup white Sobe piña colada–flavored drink

1 cup green G2 Gatorade

## INSTRUCTIONS

1. In a tall drinking glass, fill it one-third of the way with cran-apple juice.

2. Next, fill the glass to the top with ice; then, very SLOWLY pour the white Sobe drink DIRECTLY OVER the ice. Do the exact same for the green drink.

# Homemade Hot Cocoa with Candy Canes

**Prep time: 10 min**

*One of my favorite drinks during the Christmas holiday is homemade hot cocoa. It brings back wonderful memories of decorating our Christmas tree when I was young while mom was in the kitchen conjuring up wonderful homemade cocoa and toast for dunking. Yep, I'm a toast dunker.*

## INGREDIENTS

¾ cup unsweetened cocoa powder

1¼ cups powdered sugar

2¼ cups powdered milk, sifted

½ cup powdered creamer

½ teaspoon salt

1 candy cane, powdered in a blender

garnish with whipped cream or marshmallows (optional)

## INSTRUCTIONS

1. Sift together cocoa powder, powdered sugar, powdered milk, creamer, and salt into an extra large mixing bowl, stirring until well blended. By sifting the ingredients, it makes the cocoa mix smoother.

2. Add candy cane to a blender and pulse until it becomes a fine powder. Pour into cocoa ingredients and stir until well incorporated.

3. To make: Pour 1 cup boiling hot water into ⅓ cup cocoa mix. Stir together until smooth and creamy. Top with whipped cream or marshmallows, if desired.

## Mexican Hot Chocolate

1. Add 1 teaspoon ground cinnamon to cocoa ingredients and mix well.

# Slow Cooker Hot Apple Cider

Prep time: 10 min
Cook time: 2 hours
Yield: 16 servings

*While I love a hot drink of cocoa on cold winter days, there is nothing more heart-warming than a hot mug of apple cider that has brewed all day in the slow cooker and which makes your house smell like home-sweet-home. I love having this drink ready on Christmas day to sup on after we've opened our gifts. Nothing beats it.*

## INGREDIENTS

1 gallon apple cider

½ cup real maple syrup

6–8 cinnamon sticks

20 whole cloves

20 whole allspice berries

4 orange slices

1 lemon slice

cheesecloth and baker's twine

## INSTRUCTIONS

1. Pour apple cider and maple syrup in a 5- to 7-quart slow cooker; stir.

2. Place the cinnamon sticks, cloves, and allspice berries in the center of a 7 × 7–inch square of cheesecloth. Fold up the four corners of the cheesecloth to enclose the bundle and tie up with a length of baker's twine. Place the bundle in the center of the cider mixture.

3. Add orange and lemon slices.

4. Cover and cook on high for 2 hours. Reduce to low and continue cooking until ready to serve. Remove bundle, orange and lemon slices prior to serving.

5. Place cinnamon sticks, cloves, allspice berries, orange peel, and lemon peel in the center square of cheesecloth; fold up the sides of cheesecloth to enclose the bundle, then tie it up with a length of kitchen string. Drop the spice bundle into the cider mixture.

# Lobster Bisque

Prep time: 20 min
Cook time: 20 min
Yield: 3 servings

*A little lobster bisque goes a long way... bisque is so rich and luscious. I'm not sure where I got this recipe, but it's been in the old recipe box for quite some time now. Normally bisque takes a long time to make, but this recipe is super easy and quick, and it doesn't skimp on flavor either!*

## INGREDIENTS

½ pound of lobster meat, chopped into bite-sized pieces

1 tablespoon olive oil

2 tablespoons minced shallots

2 tablespoons chopped green onions

3 garlic cloves, crushed

¼ cup white wine

2 teaspoons Worcestershire sauce

2 teaspoons Tabasco sauce

1 teaspoon dried thyme

6 tablespoons sherry cooking wine

1 teaspoon paprika

1 cup hot water

1 teaspoon lobster base (Better Than Bullion Brand works great!)

4 ounces tomato paste

2 bay leaves

2 cups heavy whipping cream

4 tablespoons butter

## INSTRUCTIONS

1. Warm oil in a skillet over medium heat and sauté shallots and onions until translucent. Add garlic and continue cooking until fragrant.

2. Deglaze* pan with white wine, then stir in Worcestershire sauce, tabasco, and thyme and cook for one minute. Deglaze the pan again but this time with sherry cooking wine. Add paprika, hot water, and lobster base and mix until well blended. Stir in tomato paste. Add bay leaves and simmer for 10 minutes.

3. Remove from heat and allow to rest for 10 minutes before transferring to a blender to puree in batches. Return soup to pot. Whisk in cream and butter and turn heat up to medium high and bring soup to a boil. Reduce heat to low, stir in lobster and simmer until cooked through, stirring often. Serve while warm.

*NOTE: *Deglaze is a fancy word for simply pouring cold liquid into a very hot pan to get up all the brown bits stuck to the bottom of the pan. The "brown bits" is where all the flavors lie.*

Prep time: 15 min
Cook time: 15 min
Yield: 30 meatballs

# Ground Chicken Zucchini Meatballs

*This is a great lean and mean meatball recipe that can be used in sandwiches, on top of spaghetti all covered in cheese, or jazzed up any way you like with sauces. They're even good just plain! Really, there is no end in sight to the amount of crazy things you can do with them.*

## INGREDIENTS

1 ½ pounds ground chicken

½ cup unseasoned dry breadcrumbs

½ cup grated Parmesan cheese

½ medium onion, finely chopped

¼ cup coarsely shredded carrot

¼ cup coarsely shredded zucchini

¼ cup finely chopped flat-leaf parsley

1 teaspoon chopped fresh oregano leaves (about 1 small sprig)

¼ teaspoon salt

¼ teaspoon pepper

1 large egg white

2 garlic cloves, minced or pressed

2 teaspoons Worcestershire sauce

## INSTRUCTIONS

1. Preheat oven to 400 degrees Fahrenheit. Prepare a broiler pan with a coat of cooking spray.

2. In a large bowl, combine all ingredients until well blended. Form into 1 ½-inch meatballs. Transfer to prepared broiler pan and bake for 15 minutes or until firm and cooked through.

3. Serve with your favorite sauce (Rhu's marinara sauce has the perfect amount of spiciness for this recipe).

# Marinated Cheese Appetizers

**Prep time: 20 min + time to soak**

*I've got to tell you about my favorite thing ever…marinated cheese! Loads and loads of cheese. The cheese is marinated overnight so that all of the herbs and seasonings meld into one big hunk of flavor that I can't explain in words. It's too good for words. You'll just have to try it for yourself.*

## INGREDIENTS

¼ cup olive oil

 teaspoon sugar

¾ teaspoon dried basil

Salt and pepper, to taste

⅛ teaspoon onion powder

3 garlic cloves, minced or pressed

1 (2-ounce) jar pimentos, drained

3 tablespoons chopped fresh flat-leaf parsley

3 tablespoons chopped green onion

¼ cup balsamic vinegar

8 ounce block sharp cheddar cheese, cut into ¼-inch slices and halved

8 ounce cream cheese block, chilled, cut into ¼-inch slices, and halved

## INSTRUCTIONS

1. In a small mixing bowl, whisk together all ingredients minus the cheese.

2. Alternate cheese slices on end in a small serving dish.

3. Pour marinade over cheese, cover with plastic wrap, and refrigerate overnight.

4. Serve with crackers, crostinis, or sliced baguettes.

NOTE: *For optimal flavor, allow marinade to sit for an hour to allow flavors to meld together before slicing and pouring over cheese. If you are concerned about the acidity of the red cooking wine, the cheese offsets the acidity.*

# Divine Entrées

# Pan-Fried Halibut with Lemon Butter Sauce

Prep time: 15 min
Cook time: 15 min

*We don't eat fish that often, but when we do, this dish is one of our family's favorites. The most important part about this dish? You'd think it would be the fish, but nope, it's the lemon butter sauce! Oh my. It's like the condiment of the gods. It is so fabulous. And it's not even that big of a deal to make . . . just a splash of this, a splash of that, some seasonings, cream and butter and I've died and gone to heaven. Seriously. Died.*

*This recipe is versatile enough to use with a variety of fish you desire—like flounder, cod, trout, salmon or your favorite. We used halibut for this recipe. Halibut doesn't have a strong fishy taste so when it is dipped in this lemon butter sauce it's spot on.*

## INGREDIENTS

### LEMON BUTTER SAUCE

1 cup white cooking wine

½ cup lemon juice

1 tablespoon minced garlic

1 tablespoon minced shallots

1 teaspoon salt

¼ teaspoon black pepper

dash of Worcestershire sauce

dash hot red pepper sauce

½ cup heavy cream

1 cup butter, chopped

### FISH SPICE BLEND

½ tablespoon paprika

½ tablespoon salt

½ tablespoon garlic powder

¼ tablespoon black pepper

¼ tablespoon onion powder

¼ tablespoon cayenne pepper

¼ tablespoon dried oregano

¼ tablespoon dried thyme

½ cup flour

### FISH

2 pounds halibut or fish of choice

2 tablespoons olive oil

chopped fresh parsley to garnish

# INSTRUCTIONS

## LEMON BUTTER SAUCE

1. Warm a large skillet over medium high heat. Add cooking wine, lemon juice, garlic, and shallots and sauté for approximately three minutes. Stir in salt, pepper, Worcestershire, and hot sauce. Simmer for approximately three minutes.

2. Stir in cream and continue cooking for one minute more. Reduce to low heat. Add butter to the sauce a little at a time and whisk until well combined. Keep warm until ready to use.

## FISH

1. Whisk together spice blend with flour; set aside.

2. Warm oil in a large skillet over medium heat. Add fish to the pan and pan fry for approximately 4 minutes on each side or until cooked through.

3. Divide fish onto individual plates and spoon lemon butter sauce over the top. Garnish with fresh parsley, if desired.

# Cola Pineapple Glazed Ham

Prep time: 15 min

Cook time: 15 min per pound

Yield: 20 servings

*I consider ham to be a beautiful centerpiece for Christmas dinner. This recipe has so few ingredients but the ham is still full of great flavor. The acidity in the Cola tenderizes the meat making it "just right"! Even Goldilocks would approve!*

## INGREDIENTS

### HAM
11- to 12-pound bone-in ham with natural juices

1½ cups grape juice, divided

1½ cups cola, divided

toothpicks

### GLAZE
1 cup grape juice

1 cup cola

1 (20-ounce) can of sliced pineapple, juice reserved

2 cups packed brown sugar

## INSTRUCTIONS

1. Lower oven rack to bottom rung. Preheat oven to 275 degrees F. Line a roasting pan with foil.

2. If your ham isn't already scored, score the ham with a very sharp knife in a crisscross fashion to create a diamond pattern all over the ham. Scoring the ham helps the glaze seep deep into the ham to give you the maximum flavor.

3. Transfer ham to prepared roasting pan and pour in 1½ cups cola, 1½ cups grape juice and additional water, if needed, to bring the liquid to ½-inch high. Cover tightly with foil and cook for 2¾ or 3 hours (about 15 minutes per pound) or until a meat thermometer inserted into the thickest part of the meat (not touching bone) registers 100 degrees F.

4. Increase oven temperature to 425 degrees F. Remove ham from oven and coat with ¼ of glaze. Using toothpicks, pin down sliced pineapple to ham. Return ham to oven, uncovered. Bake for 15 minutes or until a meat thermometer registers an internal temperature of 140 degrees F.

5. Remove from oven and let rest for 15 minutes before serving. Warm up remaining glaze and drizzle over individual slices of ham.

## GLAZE

1. In a saucepan over medium-high heat, mix together grape juice, cola, pineapple juice, and brown sugar and bring to a boil. Immediately reduce heat to low and simmer for 20 minutes or until sauce is thick and glossy.

2. Remove from heat and cool to room temperature. As the sauce cools, it will thicken even more.

# Roasted Rack
of Lamb

**Prep time: 20 min**
**Cook time: 20 min**
**Yield: 4 servings**

*When thinking of an entrée to make for Christmas, many people overlook the rack of lamb. It's a wonderful alternative to your traditional meats. Rosemary's fresh, herby flavor in this recipe goes beautifully with the taste of lamb. And if you like to dip your meat, try serving it with mint sauce.*

## INGREDIENTS

½ cup dry bread crumbs

2 tablespoons minced garlic

2 tablespoons chopped fresh rosemary

2 teaspoons salt, divided

1¼ teaspoon ground black pepper, divided

4 tablespoons olive oil, divided

1 (7-bone) rack of lamb, trimmed of fat

1 tablespoon Dijon mustard

## INSTRUCTIONS

1. Move oven rack to center of oven. Preheat oven to 450 degrees F.

2. Mix together bread crumbs, garlic, rosemary, 1 teaspoon salt, and ¼ teaspoon pepper. Whisk in 2 tablespoons olive oil until moistened; set aside.

3. With remaining salt and pepper, season rack of lamb all over.

4. Warm 2 tablespoons olive oil over high heat. Add lamb and sear on both sides for 1 to 2 minutes. Remove from heat and brush lamb with mustard and dredge in bread crumb mixture. Cover end of bones with foil to prevent charring.

5. Roast in oven, fatty side up, for 12 to 18 minutes or until done. Remove from oven, cover loosely with foil, and let rest for 5 minutes before carving between ribs. Try serving with mint sauce for a little extra flavor.

# Herbed Prime Rib

**Prep time: 15 min**
**Cook time: 2 hours**
**Yield: 8–10 servings**

*This is the perfect way to wow your guests at Christmas. Prime rib is a tradition in our home for Christmas dinner. I think everyone would faint if they showed up to our home and we had something else on the table. This recipe has been perfected with time. All you have to do is create a fabulous herbed rub, season the meat, and leave it in the oven to do its magic. The meat turns out perfectly: medium-rare with a nice pink center.*

## INGREDIENTS

4 to 6 pounds rib eye roast

2½ cups beef stock

4 teaspoons salt

1¼ teaspoons ground black pepper

1 tablespoon dry ground mustard

1 teaspoon granulated garlic

1 teaspoon granulated onion powder

½ teaspoon dried thyme leaves

½ teaspoon dried oregano

½ teaspoon ground coriander

½ teaspoon whole celery seeds

1 tablespoon olive oil

## INSTRUCTIONS

1. Preheat oven to 325 degrees F. Line a roasting pan with foil and pour in beef stock; set aside.

2. **To make herbed rub:** In a small bowl whisk together salt and pepper, dry mustard, granulated garlic, onion powder, thyme, oregano, coriander, and celery seeds until well blended; set aside.

3. Using a sharp knife, make 6 small slits along the fat side of the roast to about 1½-inch depth. Rub olive oil all over roast.

4. Sprinkle rub evenly over roast. Rub it in with your fingers, pressing down as you go. Make sure to rub it in and around the slits. The slits will allow the herbs to penetrate the roast.

5. Place the roast fat-side up in prepared roasting pan with beef stock. Cook uncovered for approximately 1¾ hours to 2¾ hours (depending on poundage) or until a meat thermometer registers 135 F for medium-rare and 150 F for medium.

6. Remove from oven, cover with foil and allow to sit 15 minutes before carving and serving.

NOTE: *Serve with au jus sauce or a creamed mixture of 1 cup sour cream, 1 tablespoon horseradish, 1 tablespoon finely chopped green onion, 2 teaspoons Dijon mustard, 2 teaspoons white wine vinegar, and ¼ teaspoon salt.*

# Perfect
# Pot Roast

**Prep time: 20 min**
**Cook time: 3 hours**
**Yield: 4–6 servings**

*The best cut of meat for your pot roast is chuck roast. The great thing about this recipe is its versatility; you can make this roast for the oven or for the slow cooker. You may have to cut back on adding vegetables if you use the slow cooker so you don't over stuff it. If you use the slow cooker, cook on low for 8 hours. Plan on cooking the roast low and slow—you can't rush a good thing—and by the time it is finished, it will be so tender it will melt in your mouth.*

## INGREDIENTS

3- to 4-pound boneless chuck roast

2 teaspoons salt

1 teaspoon ground black pepper

½ teaspoon garlic powder

2 teaspoons herbs de Provence

2 to 3 tablespoons olive oil

2 onions, peeled and halved.

1 to 2 cups baby-cut carrots

4–6 Russet or Yukon gold potatoes, peeled and quartered

1 cup red cooking wine

2 tablespoons Worcestershire sauce

3 cups beef broth

2 to 3 sprigs fresh rosemary

2 to 3 sprigs fresh thyme

### GRAVY

3 cups reserved liquid

2 tablespoons corn starch

1/4 cup cold water

## INSTRUCTIONS

1.  Preheat oven to 275 degrees F. Line the bottom of a roasting pan with foil; set aside.

2.  Mix together salt, pepper, garlic powder, and herbs de Provence and rub half or more of the seasoning into the roast on all sides. Heat olive oil in a large skillet over medium-high heat and lightly sear roast about one minute on all sides until lightly browned all over. Remove and place in prepared roasting pan.

3.  In same skillet, add more olive oil if needed. When warmed, add quartered onions and potatoes, sprinkle with remaining seasoning, and lightly brown on all sides. Transfer vegetables and carrots to roasting pan and place around the roast.

4. Combine cooking wine, Worcestershire sauce and beef broth into a large bowl. Pour over pot roast. Top with herbs and bay leaves. Cover with foil or lid and roast for 3 to 3½ hours or until it falls apart and is tender.

## GRAVY

1. Remove meat and vegetables from pan and pour liquid into a saucepan. Bring to a boil.
2. In a small bowl, whisk together corn starch and water. Pour mixture into liquid to thicken gravy; stirring constantly.

# Pork Tenderloin

**Prep time: 15 min**
**Cook time: 30 min**
**Yield: 3–4 servings**

*If you don't cook pork right, it can be very dry! It's one of those meats that is easy to overcook and, of course, we want a "tender" loin (pun intended). The key to making tenderloin? Patience. Slather on plenty of seasoning and that hunk of meat will end up tender, juicy, and full of flavor. It will satisfy the carnivore in you. Pinky swear.*

## INGREDIENTS

1 teaspoon garlic powder

1 teaspoon dried oregano

1 teaspoon ground cumin

1 teaspoon ground coriander

1 teaspoon dried thyme

salt, to taste

1 tablespoon olive oil

1 teaspoon minced garlic

1½ pounds pork tenderloin, extra fat trimmed

½ cup red cooking wine

½ cup low-sodium chicken stock

## INSTRUCTIONS

1. Preheat oven to 400 degrees F.

2. Whisk together seasonings (minus the olive oil, meat, and minced garlic) until well blended to form a rub.

3. With dry hands, sprinkle rub all over the tenderloin pressing down as you go to adhere seasoning to the tenderloin.

4. In a large oven-proof skillet over medium-high heat, warm oil. Add minced garlic and sauté until flavorful and aromatic (about 1 minute). Add tenderloin to skillet and sear all sides of the meat until golden (about 1 to 2 minutes per side). Turn off heat and whisk in cooking wine and chicken stock.

5. Transfer skillet to the oven and roast for 30–40 minutes, or until a meat thermometer inserted registers 170 degrees F. Let the pork rest for 10 minutes before slicing and serving.

# Festive Sides

# Mom's Creamy Cherry Whip Salad

**Prep time: 15 min**
**Yield: 15 servings**

*This is a recipe that has been gracing our table since I've been a young girl (which is about two years ago . . . cough, cough) and it's from my mom. Every holiday mom whips up this creamy cherry dish and each time we empty the bowl, lick our spoons and we might even lower ourselves to licking our plates. Just saying. Mom doesn't measure out a thing when she makes this salad. She's been making it for 30 or so years and she has it completely memorized. And while the alterations may be slight, the taste is always incredible!*

## INGREDIENTS

3 ounces cream cheese, softened

1 can sweetened condensed milk

1 (21-ounce) can of cherry pie filling & topping

1 (15-ounce) can crushed pineapple, drained

12 ounces frozen whipped cream topping, thawed

crushed walnuts (optional)

## INSTRUCTIONS

1. In a large mixing bowl, beat together cream cheese and sweetened condensed milk until smooth and creamy. Stir in cherry pie filling and crushed pineapples. Fold in Cool Whip and crushed walnuts.

2. Pour into a 9 × 13–inch pan and refrigerate for 2 hours or overnight before serving.

# Herbed Fingerling Potatoes

**Prep time: 5 min**
**Cook time: 25 min**
**Yield: 4–6 servings**

*Sometimes mashed potatoes and gravy just won't do and these fingerling potatoes are a fun alternative. I've always said anything "miniature" is so cute and so are these fingerlings. I like to use two or three different colored fingerling potatoes to make this dish look pretty, but you don't have to.*

## INGREDIENTS

1 teaspoon coarse salt

½ teaspoon ground black pepper

1½ teaspoons Herbes de Provence

1½ to 2 pounds fingerling potatoes, scrubbed (I like using different varieties of fingerling potatoes)

1 tablespoon extra-virgin olive oil

3 cloves garlic, minced or pressed

## INSTRUCTIONS

1. In a small bowl, mix together salt, pepper, and herbes de Provence until well blended; set aside.

2. Place potatoes in a large bowl, drizzle with olive oil, sprinkle in garlic, and toss to completely coat potatoes.

3. Generously sprinkle half of the seasoned-salt mixture over potatoes, toss, and sprinkle remaining amount over potatoes and toss again.

4. Place potatoes in a single layer on a foil-lined baking sheet and roast for 25-30 minutes, turning occasionally, until tender when pricked with a fork.

5. Remove and serve while warm.

# Gifts From the Kitchen

**Prep time: 15 min**
**Cook time: 35 min**
**Yield: 15 servings**

# Red Velvet Oreo Fudge Brownies

*Can you say "heaven"? These Red Velvet Oreo Fudge Brownies stole my heart and have been the gateway to falling in love with red velvet. These are the brownies you make when your boyfriend breaks up with you, or when you don't land the gig you want, or when it's raining instead of sunny, or because it is sunny instead of raining, or just because you received the Christmas present you always wanted!*

*I've lightened up this recipe by using applesauce instead of butter, plain Greek yogurt instead of oil, and low-fat cream cheese. Believe me, your hips will thank me later. You may need to unbuckle your belt or put on some stretchy pants for this one. Totally worth it though!*

## INGREDIENTS

1 Duncan Hines Red Velvet Cake Mix

1 (3.3-ounce) package Jell-O instant white chocolate pudding mix

½ cup butter

6 tablespoons oil

2 eggs, separated

1 (13.3-ounce) package Oreo cookies

8 ounces low-fat cream cheese

1½ cups semisweet chocolate chips

1 tablespoon butter or shortening

½ cup semisweet mini chocolate chips to garnish (optional)

## INSTRUCTIONS

1. Preheat oven to 325 degrees F. Line a 9 × 13–inch baking pan with parchment paper and lightly coat with cooking spray. I'm a parchment freak. It's easier clean up, but if you don't have parchment on hand, just spray the pan with a light coating of cooking spray.

2. Beat together cake mix, pudding mix, butter, oil, and egg yolks.

3. In a separate mixing bowl, beat the egg whites with an electric mixer on high until they form a stiff peak. Fold into batter. Beat batter on medium speed until smooth. The batter will be extremely thick. This is normal. Spread the batter the best to your ability in the prepared baking dish. Use the back of a lightly oiled spoon, spreading and smoothing out.

4. Bake for 35–38 minutes or until a toothpick poked in the center comes out clean. Check the brownies after 20–25 minutes. Altitude and ovens bake differently and you may need to adjust the time.

5. Remove from oven, let slightly cool on a baking rack, and place in the refrigerator to cool completely.

6. Meanwhile, place Oreos in a food processor or blender and blend until cookies become small crumbs; pour into a small bowl.

7. Stir together Oreo crumbs and softened cream cheese until well combined. Spoon dollops of the Oreo mixture across the surface of the red velvet brownies and gently spread the mixture.

8. Place chocolate chips in a small microwave-safe bowl and top with butter or shortening. Microwave for 30 seconds on high. Stir. Repeat for 30 more seconds or until the chocolate has melted. Stir until completely smooth. Pour and spread over the top of Oreo mixture and garnish with mini chocolate chips while the chocolate is still warm.

9. Place in the refrigerator to cool completely before cutting into bars and serving.

# Cathedral Windows

Prep time: 15 min

Cook time: 5 min

Total time: 20 min
+ 2 hours for setting

Yield: 3 dozen

*I'm embarrassed to admit that I came out of the store with TWO bags of mini colored marshmallows. Why TWO? It's quite simple . . . How can you make these candies and not suck down a bunch of marshmallows along the way? These marshmallows are eye candy for the holidays, and my inner seven-year-old thought they screamed out "eat me." Which I did. Don't judge me. Adding chocolate was the icing on the cake.*

## INGREDIENTS

½ cup butter

12 ounces semisweet chocolate chips

1 teaspoon pure vanilla extract

1 cup chopped almonds

1 (10-ounce) package multi-colored miniature marshmallows

2 cups sweetened coconut flakes

## INSTRUCTIONS

1. In a large saucepan over low heat, melt together butter and chocolate chips; stir until smooth and creamy. Remove from heat and stir in vanilla. Let cool slightly.

2. In a large bowl, toss together marshmallows, almonds, and chocolate mixture until well coated.

3. Tear off five 9-inch sheets of waxed paper and lay out on counter. Generously sprinkle each sheet with coconut. Divide chocolate mixture between waxed paper. Spoon the mixture in the shape of a log down the center of the wax paper. Roll tightly into logs and twist ends to seal. Refrigerate overnight or until firm.

4. Before serving, unwrap from waxed paper and cut into ¾-inch slices.

# Overnight Butter Pecan Cookies

Prep time: 45 min
+ overnight
refrigeration
Cook time: 15 min
Yield: 75–80 cookies

*I always like to keep a bag of pecans on hand for snacking and cooking. I love them chopped up in salads, ice cream, cakes, etc. So it's no surprise that these pecans wound up in a batch of my butter cookies. I love cookies—I am my own Cookie Monster. I like my cookies soft and chewy or crunchy, and these butter pecan cookies are somewhere in between.*

## INGREDIENTS

2 cups flour

1¼ cups pecans, chopped and lightly toasted

½ teaspoon salt

3 sticks unsalted butter, softened

1 cup + 2 tablespoons powdered sugar

1 tablespoon pure vanilla extract

## INSTRUCTIONS

1. In a large mixing bowl, stir together flour, pecans, and salt; set aside.

2. In a separate bowl, beat together butter, powdered sugar, and vanilla until smooth and creamy.

3. Add the flour mixture to the butter mixture and stir together until incorporated.

4. Divide dough in two and place each on a lightly floured sheet of wax paper. Refrigerate for 30–60 minutes or until stiff enough to shape into logs.

5. Remove from refrigerator and roll each dough into a log approximately 10 inches long and 1¼ inches round. Wrap again in waxed paper of plastic wrap and refrigerate overnight.

6. Preheat oven to 350 degrees F. Grease or line a baking sheet with parchment paper.

7. Slice logs into ¼-inch slices and place 2 inches apart on prepared baking sheet. Bake 15–17 minutes or until edges begin to turn a golden brown. Remove and place on a baking rack before serving.

# Collin's Marshmallow Fudge

Prep time: 10 min

Cook time: 5 min

Total time: 15 min
+ 2 hours chilling

Yield: 50 (1-inch) pieces

*Don't you just love hair dressers? They are great therapy! I have the best hairdresser, Collin.*

*Collin has cut my hair for over ten years and we've become fast friends. He makes me laugh—not just a small giggle, but that kind of laugh that comes deep from the belly, where you feel like you can't catch your breath. That's my Collin. He's been through everything with me and he still wants to cut my hair knowing just how dysfunctional I am. On top of all that, Collin is a fantastic cook and always has my mouth drooling with the latest dishes he and his spouse concoct. One such recipe is this marshmallow fudge. After I got the recipe, I was like a puppy wagging my tail in delight to get home and try it out. It was delicious. So it's no surprise to find it here in this recipe book.*

## INGREDIENTS

3 cups granulated sugar

1½ sticks (1¼ cup) butter, chopped

6 ounces evaporated milk (do not use sweetened condensed milk)

6 ounces semisweet chocolate chips (Ghirardelli)

5 ounces bittersweet chocolate (Ghirardelli 60% cacao)

1 (7-ounce) jar marshmallow crème

½–1 cup chopped pecans or walnuts (optional)

1 teaspoon pure vanilla extract

## INSTRUCTIONS

1. Line a 9 × 13–inch pan with foil and grease the foil with butter.

2. In a heavy saucepan, bring sugar, butter, milk, and marshmallow crème to a rolling boil over high heat, stirring constantly. Reduce heat to medium and boil gently for 5 minutes, stirring constantly.

3. Remove from heat and stir in chocolate chips, marshmallow crème, nuts, and vanilla. Stir until chocolate and crème are melted.

4. Pour into prepared pan and cool completely in the fridge until firm. Remove from pan and foil and cut into 1-inch squares.

Prep time: 5 min
Cook time: 8–10 min
Yield: 18 cups

# Gary's Gooey Caramel Popcorn

*This is THE best and simplest caramel popcorn: a treat that our kids beg my husband to make while watching a movie or having sleepovers at the house. It's gobbled up so quickly, no kernel is left behind. It's sinfully delicious.*

## INGREDIENTS

1 can of sweetened condensed milk

2 cups brown sugar, firmly packed

½ cup butter or margarine

1 cup light corn syrup

a pinch of salt

18 cups cooked popcorn (or 3 bags of microwave popcorn, popped)

## INSTRUCTIONS

1. Cook all ingredients in a large, heavy saucepan on medium heat to soft ball stage or about 235 degrees F. (If you don't have a candy thermometer, you can test the candy by dropping a little mixture in cold water. If it forms a soft ball, it's done.)

2. Pour over popcorn and mix with a wooden spoon until evenly coated.

3. Eat as is or form into balls and store in a covered container.

TIP: *Add a cup of peanuts for crunchy texture and salty flavor. There's something about sweet and salty that's so divine.*

# Santa's Whiskers

Prep time: 15 min
+ refrigeration
Cook time: 12 min
Yield: 2 dozen

*These cookies are old-fashioned cookies that have been around forever! They are perfect for Christmas. Just wait till you taste these cherry-filled cookies rolled up in Santa's whiskers (coconut). They are a nice addition for gifts on a plate.*

## INGREDIENTS

½ cup butter, softened

½ cup granulated sugar

1 large egg, beaten

1 tablespoon milk

½ teaspoon pure vanilla extract

1½ cups flour

¼ cup dried cranberries, finely chopped

¼ cup pecans, finely chopped

½ cup sweetened coconut flakes

## INSTRUCTIONS

1. In a large mixing bowl, beat together butter, sugar, and egg until creamy and fluffy. Add in milk and vanilla.

2. Slowly add in flour ½ cup at a time and stir well with each new addition. Fold in chopped cherries and pecans.

3. Divide dough and shape into two 7-inch rolls. Roll in coconut, wrap in wax paper, and chill for several hours.

4. Preheat oven to 375 degrees F. Cut into ¼-inch slices. Place on an ungreased baking sheet and bake for 10–12 minutes or until done.

# Raspberry Pecan Bars

Prep: 20 min
Bake: 10 min
+ cooling
Yield: 12 servings

*Raspberry pecan bars taste just like a berry patch, and really any berry can be substituted. I've tried it with blueberries and blueberry preserves, which was truly amazing.*

## INGREDIENTS

⅔ cup ground pecans

½ cup graham cracker crumbs

2 tablespoons + ⅓ cup sugar

⅓ cup old-fashioned oats

3 tablespoons butter, melted

8 ounces cream cheese

1 tablespoon orange juice

½ teaspoon vanilla extract

½ cup prepared whipped topping

2 tablespoon raspberry preserves

1½ cups fresh raspberries

## INSTRUCTIONS

1. Combine pecans, cracker crumbs, 2 tablespoons sugar, oats, and butter. Press onto the bottom of an 8-inch square baking dish coated with cooking spray. Bake at 350 for 9–11 minutes or until set and edges are lightly browned. Cool on a wire rack.

2. In a large bowl, beat cream cheese and remaining sugar until smooth. Beat in orange juice and vanilla. Fold in whipped topping. Spread over crust.

3. In a microwave-safe bowl, heat preserves on high for 15–20 seconds or until warmed; gently stir in raspberries. Spoon over filling. Refrigerate until serving.

# Auntie M's Infamous Toffee

Prep time: 20 min
Cook time: 10 min
Yield: about 40 pieces

*When I say "Auntie M," I'm not talking about Dorothy's Auntie Em on* The Wizard of Oz. *No, we have our very own special and loving Auntie M, and she makes the most incredible toffee. We look forward to her yearly package of toffee and fudge at Christmas time. We love that sweet, salty, buttery crunch of toffee. Fair warning . . . it's addictive and it's known to make your clothes shrink.*

## INGREDIENTS

1 cup sugar

1 cup butter

2 tablespoons cold water

a dash of salt

1 teaspoon vanilla extract

1 (12-ounce) bag semisweet or milk chocolate chips

1 cup chopped pecans

## INSTRUCTIONS

1. Generously coat a 9 × 13–inch baking pan with butter

2. Combine sugar, butter, and water in a large, heavy saucepan over medium-high heat. Bring to a boil, stirring constantly so it doesn't crystallize.

3. Clamp a candy thermometer to the side of the saucepan, making sure it doesn't touch the bottom of the pan. Cook, without stirring, until mixture reaches 300 degrees F ("hard crack" stage) on the thermometer.

4. Immediately remove from heat and stir in salt and vanilla.

5. Pour mixture immediately into prepared pan and spread with a buttered spatula.

6. Top with chocolate chips over hot mixture. After a few minutes, chocolate will be soft enough to spread with a buttered spatula or back of a buttered spoon.

7. Sprinkle crushed pecans over the top of melted chocolate.

8. Cool completely and break into pieces once hardened.

9. Store in an airtight container at room temperature or refrigerator up to 10 days.

# Giant Ginger Cookies

**Prep time:** 10 min

**Cook time:**
12–14 min

**Yield:** 1 dozen giant
or 2 dozen
regular size

*As I mentioned before, I am my own Cookie Monster, and the thing I love about these ginger cookies is that I don't have to roll them out and cut them out to look like little men. Believe me, that is a huge time saver. This cookie recipe makes one dozen giant cookies. So let's do the math . . . If I had 12 cookies and you took one, what would you have? That's correct . . . a black eye and a broken hand. I'm very protective of my food.*

## INGREDIENTS

2¼ cups flour

2 teaspoons ground ginger

1 teaspoons baking soda

¾ teaspoon ground cinnamon

½ teaspoon ground cloves

⅛ teaspoon salt

¾ cup shortening

1 cup granulated sugar

1 egg

¼ cup molasses

½ cup coarse sugar or granulated sugar, to roll dough in

## INSTRUCTIONS

1. Preheat oven to 350 degrees F.

2. Mix together flour, ginger, baking soda, cinnamon, cloves, and salt in a medium mixing bowl.

3. In a separate bowl, beat together shortening and sugar. Add eggs and molasses and continue beating until smooth and creamy. Add a little flour at a time and continue beating in as much as you can until it gets too stiff for the mixture. Fold in any remaining flour.

4. Using ¼ cup dough, shape into 2-inch balls. Roll in sugar and place 2½ inches apart on an ungreased cookie sheet. Bake for 12 to 14 minutes or until light brown and puffy. Do not overbake or they will harden and not be chewy.

5. Let cookies cool slightly on cookie sheet (about 2 minutes) before transferring to a wire rack to cool completely. Store in an airtight container up to 5 days or in the freezer for 3 months.

# Christmas Cinnamon-Sugar Roasted Almonds

**Prep time: 10 min**
**Cook time: 1 hour**
**Yield: 16 servings**

*I love the Christmas season—the sights, the sounds, the smells are uh-mazing. I enjoy walking through the malls and smelling the wonderful scent of cinnamon-sugar roasted almonds. My mouth literally waters—like my dog's as he rests his head on my lap begging and drooling for a morsel to eat. These almonds are fabulous for snacking or even adding to your green salads. WARNING: Once you pop it in your mouth, you won't be able to stop! It's almost guaranteed that once you eat one, it will turn into two, three, or even a hundred almonds in your mouth.*

## INGREDIENTS

1 egg white

1 teaspoon pure vanilla extract

4 cups whole almonds

1 teaspoon ground cinnamon

¼ teaspoon salt

⅓ cup sugar

⅓ cup brown sugar

## INSTRUCTIONS

1. Preheat oven to 250 degrees F. Line a baking sheet with parchment paper and lightly coat with cooking spray.

2. Whisk together egg white and vanilla until frothy. Stir in almonds until almonds are completely coated; set aside.

3. In a medium bowl, mix together sugars, salt, and cinnamon. Fold in almond mixture and mix until almonds are completed coated.

4. Transfer to prepared baking sheet and spread in an even layer. Cook for one hour, gently turning over with a spatula every 20 minutes.

5. Remove from oven and allow to cool completely before serving. Store in an airtight container.

**Prep time: 20 min**
**Cook time: 22 min**
**Yield: 1 (2-layer) cake**

# Red Velvet Peppermint Cake

*There is so much to love about red velvet! Not only is the color beautiful, but the buttermilk and cocoa go a long way to making this a moist and luscious cake. I have a friend who makes the best red velvet cakes and I've learned a lot from her. I'm not certain she'd approve of me using premade cake mixes in this recipe, but hey, if it doesn't scrimp on taste, why not? Oh, and you'll love—LOVE—the peppermint flavored frosting. The bomb dot com.*

## INGREDIENTS

### CAKE

1 (18.25-ounce) package white cake mix

3 egg whites

1⅓ cups buttermilk

2 tablespoons vegetable oil

1 (9-ounce) package yellow cake mix

½ cup buttermilk

1 large egg

1½ tablespoons cocoa

½ teaspoon baking soda

2 tablespoons liquid red food coloring

1 teaspoon cider vinegar

peppermint cream cheese frosting (recipe follows)

peppermint candies, to garnish (optional)

two 9-inch cake pans

### FROSTING

1 (8-ounce) package cream cheese, softened

1 cup butter or margarine, softened

1 (2-pound) package powdered sugar

2 teaspoons peppermint extract

## INSTRUCTIONS

### CAKE

1. Preheat oven to 350 degrees F. Grease and flour two 9-inch cake pans; set aside.

2. Beat together white cake mix, egg whites, buttermilk and vegetable oil with an electric mixer on medium speed.

3. In a separate bowl, beat together yellow cake mix, buttermilk, egg, cocoa, baking soda, red food coloring, and vinegar with an electric mixer on medium speed.

4. Evenly divide white cake mix between prepared cake pans. Spoon red cake mix in dollops over top of white cake batter in both pans. With a knife, gently swirl red batter throughout white batter.

5. Bake for 22 to 25 minutes or until a toothpick entered into the center of the cakes come out clean. Cool pans on a wire rack for 10 minutes before turning out on wire racks to cool completely.

6. Generously layer frosting to top of one cake, layer with second cake. Gently spread frosting on top and sides of cake, using swirling motions as you go. Stick peppermint candies to frosting all around the bottom of the cake. Reserve a couple of candies to crush and sprinkle on top.

7. Cake may be refrigerated up to two days or frozen up to one month before frosting.

## FROSTING

1. With an electric mixer on medium speed, beat together cream cheese and butter until creamy. Reduce speed to low and gradually add in sugar until creamy and smooth; scraping down sides as you go. Add extract and continue beating until well blended.

# Funfetti Cookies

**Prep time: 15 min**

**Cook time: 8 min**

**Yield: 2½ dozen cookies**

*Looking at these cookies, it definitely looks like a par-tay is waiting to happen.*

*Have you noticed that cookie recipes are proportionately made so we eat only as much as we should—which is only ONE rounded cookie? That just isn't right, don't you think? I have been known to polish off half a dozen cookies by myself in one sitting!*

*These are the perfect cookies to bring along to a potluck or bake sale. But you can also eat them alone and have your own little party.*

## INGREDIENTS

2¼ cups flour

¾ teaspoon baking soda

¼ teaspoon salt

¾ cup + 2 tablespoons unsalted butter, softened

1¼ cups granulated sugar

1 large egg

1 large egg yolk

1 teaspoon vanilla extract

¾ teaspoon almond extract

1 (3.5-ounce) package instant vanilla pudding mix

⅔ cup rainbow Jimmie sprinkles, plus more for topping

Funfetti frosting (optional)

## INSTRUCTIONS

1. Preheat oven to 350 degrees F. Line two baking sheets with parchment paper; set aside.

2. Whisk together flour, soda, and salt; set aside.

3. In a separate bowl, beat together butter and sugar with an electric mixer on medium speed. Beat in egg, egg yolk, vanilla extract, and almond extract. Fold in vanilla pudding mix until well blended.

4. With an electric mixer on low, gradually add in dry ingredients until well combined. Fold in sprinkles.

5. Shape dough into 1½-inch balls and place two inches apart on prepared cookie sheets. Sprinkle additional Jimmies to top of cookies. With the bottom of a glass dipped in flour, gently press down dough to about ¼ inch in thickness.

6. Bake in preheated oven for 8–10 minutes. Allow to cool on baking sheet for a few minutes before transferring to a wire rack to cool completely. If desired, top with Funfetti frosting by making your own favorite buttercream frosting and folding in Jimmies until well incorporated or simply frost cookies and sprinkle Jimmies on top.

7. Store in an airtight container (if they last that long).

1. "Autumn Potato Gratin," *Better Homes and Gardens*. http://www.bhg.com/recipe/autumn-potato-gratin/

2. "Breakfast Enchiladas," *My Recipes*. http://www.myrecipes.com/recipe/breakfast-enchiladas

3. "Caramel-Pecan Pumpkin Pie," *All Recipes*. http://allrecipes.com/Recipe/Caramel-Pecan-Pumpkin-Pie/Detail.aspx?event8=1&prop24=SR_Title&e11=caramel%20pecan%20pumpkin%20pie&e8=Quick%20Search&event10=1&e7=%2f404.aspx&soid=sr_results_p1i1

4. Danielle, "Chocolate Peanut Butter No-Bake Dessert," *Let's Dish*. Retrieved March 22, 2012. http://www.letsdishrecipes.com/2012/03/chocolate-peanut-butter-no-bake-dessert.html

5. "Giant Ginger Cookies," *Better Homes & Gardens*. http://www.bgh.com/recipe/desserts/giant-ginger-cookies/

6. "Homemade Green Bean Casserole," *Better Homes and Gardens*. http://www.bhg.com/recipe/homemade-green-bean-casserole/

7. Jaclyn, "Chicken Pot Pie Soup and parmesan Drop Biscuits," *Cooking Classy*. http://www.cookingclassy.com/2013/10/chicken-pot-pie-soup-parmesan-drop-biscuits/

8. Jaden Hair, "Cole-Pineapple Glazed Ham," *Steamy Kitchen*. http://steamykitchen.com/15072-cola-pineapple-glazed-ham-easter-recipe.html

9. Marian, "Pumpkin Cupcakes with Maple Cream Cheese Icing," *Sweetopia*. http://sweetopia.net/2012/09/pumpkin-cupcakes-with-maple-cream-cheese-icing/

10. McCormick, "Homemade Root Beer," *McCormick.com*. http://www.mccormick.com/Recipes/Beverages-Cocktails/Homemade-Root-Beer

11. Pam Brandon, "Caramel Apple Pie," *Delicious Disney Cookbook*.

12. "Pumpkin Web Tart," *Taste of Home*: Ultimate Halloween 2014: 90

13. "Red Velvet Peppermint Cake," *My Recipes*. http://www.myrecipes.com/recipe/red-velvet-peppermint-cake

14. "Thanksgiving Punch," *MyRecipes.com*. http://www.myrecipes.com/recipe/thanksgiving-punch

15. Tim Talevich, *Fabulous Food the Costco Way* (Shanghai, China: Toppan Leefung Printing, 2014), recipes found on pages 14, 18, 62, 73, 163, and 209.

About the Author

Jeni Potter Scott is the owner, author, and creative mind behind Bakerette.com, where she features daily recipes, gardening information, and DIY projects. She has been featured on KSL's Studio 5, ABC's Good Things Utah, and wowOwow.com, which was created by Whoopi Goldberg, Lily Tomlin, Candice Bergen, Lesley Stahl, and others. Jeni is also a regularly featured contributor to CookingWithRuthie.com, The36thAvenue.com, and MadeFromPinterest.net. She is a budding photographer and formerly was the photographer for AddyLou.com, a subsidiary of Modern Display.

Jeni works full time as an executive assistant and currently volunteers her time for a local botanical garden, where she serves as vice president of Jordan Valley's Home & Garden Club, the first of its kind in the nation.